W9-ACN-661

RECIPES FOR
THE PRESSURE COOKER
Revised Edition

Joanna White

BRISTOL PUBLISHING ENTERPRISES, INC.
San Leandro, California

a nitty gritty® cookbook

©1998 Bristol Publishing Enterprises, Inc., P.O. Box 1737, San Leandro, California 94577. World rights reserved. No part of this publication may be reproduced in any form nor may it be stored in a retrieval system, transmitted, or otherwise copied for public or private use without prior written permission from the publisher.

Printed in the United States of America.

ISBN 1-55867-194-3

Cover design: Frank J. Paredes
Cover photography: John A. Benson
Food stylist: Susan Massey
Illustrator: James Balkovek

CONTENTS

ABOUT PRESSURE COOKERS

I couldn't believe how quickly I could prepare meals with a pressure cooker. With the fast lifestyle of the '90s, coupled with an interest in health, pressure cooking is ideal for today's households. Contemporary pressure cookers or "supercookers," as they are sometimes called, are usually made from stainless steel and have a heavy plate welded to the bottom, which helps prevent burning and evenly distributes the heat. Several safety features are built in so that it is virtually impossible for the cooker to explode. So forget the old images of spaghetti sauce on the ceiling. Do something wonderful for your family while making your life a lot easier — invest in a pressure cooker!

ADVANTAGES OF PRESSURE COOKING

- *Pressure cooking is energy efficient*: Once the desired pressure is reached, cooking temperature increases and cooking time decreases, often as much as $1/3$ to $1/2$ the time it takes to cook conventionally.

- *Pressure cooking is cost efficient*: Since pressure cooking has a tenderizing effect on protein fibers, low-cost meats can be used.

- *Pressure cookers are versatile*: Today's pressure cookers come with trivets and steamer baskets for several different cooking options and easy removal of food.

- *Pressure cooking preserves nutrients*: Because of reduced cooking time, fewer nutrients are lost during the cooking process. Also, since the cooking container is sealed, less nutrition is lost due to evaporation.

- *Pressure cookers are safe*: Contemporary pressure cookers have multiple built-in safety features. The combination of a steam release valve, a manual pressure release valve and a lid gasket virtually eliminates the possibility of an explosion. In addition to all of the safety features, pressure will only build if the lid is properly sealed. Conversely, the lid can only be removed when no pressure remains.

- *Pressure cookers are all-purpose kitchen tools*: Pressure cookers are available in a large range of sizes. Common capacities are 4-, 6-, 8- and 10-quart. I recommend buying a larger size, because you can do more with it, including cooking casseroles, cheesecakes and custards. A pressure cooker can also be used as a conventional pot when uncovered. It works especially well when cooking large quantities of food, such as soups or stocks. You can cook small quantities in a large pressure cooker; however, the converse is not true.

HOW TO USE A PRESSURE COOKER

It is essential to consult the manufacturer's instructions for your pressure cooker before using it. It's very important to feel comfortable with how your pressure cooker works. Each make and model has specific instructions for bringing the food items up to pressure and releasing the pressure after cooking. If you have misplaced the instructions manual, call the manufacturer for a replacement. Once you are familiar with how to use it, cooking in your pressure cooker will be worry-free.

GENERAL INSTRUCTIONS

1. Sauté or brown meats or vegetables if called for in the recipe. This can be done in the pressure cooker, but take care to scrape up all of the browned bits from the bottom of the cooker to prevent burning. In many of the recipes in this book, the meats and vegetables are browned in a separate skillet and then transferred to the pressure cooker in order to prevent burning.

2. For pressure steaming or steam roasting, remove the browned item from the pressure cooker, if necessary. Place the trivet or steamer basket in the cooker. (Most pressure cookers are now sold with a trivet and/or a steamer basket. If you don't have them, substitute a metal folding steamer rack that can be found in kitchenware shops.) Place the browned item on the trivet or steamer basket.

3.   Add remaining ingredients, not exceeding the fill line, and bring to a boil. This helps to bring the cooker up to pressure rapidly, which also helps to prevent burning.

4.   Position the lid on the bottom portion of the cooker and seal it according to the manufacturer's instructions.

5.   Bring the pressure up to the desired level over high heat. Most contemporary pressure cookers feature a round pressure indicator located on the center of the lid. As pressure rises, small rings appear on the indicator, which correspond to different levels of pressure: the first ring indicates low pressure, about 5 to 8 lb.; the second ring indicates medium pressure, about 10 to 12 lb.; the third ring indicates high pressure, about 13 to 15 lb. Consult your owner's manual for specific information. Most of the recipes in this book are cooked under high pressure.

6.   Stabilize the pressure by reducing the heat on your stove to very low. If the valve begins to release steam, the pressure is too high. Start timing the recipes now.

7.   When the cooking is complete, remove the pressure cooker from the heat. Release the pressure according to manufacturer's directions and/or as directed in the recipe. There are three general methods:

Quick Release Method: Push the release valve (consult manufacturer's instructions) continually until all of the steam is released, which usually takes about 30 seconds. The lid cannot be removed until all of the steam is released. Use this method when you need to release the pressure immediately and for items that can be easily overcooked.

Cold Water Release Method: Place the cooker in the sink under a stream of cold running water. Unlock and remove the lid when the pressure indicator reverts to normal. This works well for foods that have a tendency to foam, such as beans or rice, or foods that have a lot of liquid, such as soups, stocks and applesauce.

Natural Release Method: Unlock the lid and allow the pressure to disperse naturally, which takes between 3 and 20 minutes. This works well for stews, rice, cheesecakes and meats, all of which benefit from an extra resting period.

NOTE: If the lid won't budge, it probably means there is a *vapor lock* or *vacuum lock*. If this happens, unlock the lid and return the cooker to the heat for no more than a few minutes. The lid should easily come off.

PRESSURE COOKER DO's AND DON'Ts

- If you are using an older model of pressure cooker without the built-in safety features, **always follow the instructions that are specific for that model.**

- Unless the recipe states to use the trivet or steamer basket, remove these items before cooking.

- Never exceed the fill line of your pressure cooker. Generally, this is ⅔ full. **All of the recipes in this book will work in a 6-quart or larger pressure cooker.** Keep in mind that it is easier to fit baking dishes into the larger models.

- Make sure the lid is properly secured and locked into position before bringing it up to pressure.

- Follow the manufacturer's instructions for properly cleaning your pressure cooker, paying special attention to the valves. Do not put the lid in the dishwasher, as it may damage the rubber gasket.

- Periodically check the rubber gasket to make sure it is not worn. Always store the lid upside down to prevent wear and tear of the gasket. Never place the lid on a hot stove or over a burner because the heat may damage the gasket.

- When removing the lid, follow the manufacturer's instructions. Always open the lid away from your face.

ADAPTING YOUR OWN RECIPES

- Follow *General Instructions for Pressure Cooking* on pages 3 to 5.
- In general, cut the cooking time down from 1/3 to 1/2 the cooking time in your original recipe.
- Allow 1/2 cup of liquid for each 10 minutes of cooking time. If you exceed 30 minutes of cooking time, increase the liquid by 1/2 cup. For steaming vegetables, allow 1 cup liquid for each 10 minutes of cooking. Do not exceed the maximum fill line with your total food volume, and be sure to use the minimum amount of liquid required for your particular brand of pressure cooker.
- Season dishes lightly at first, since pressure cooking retains much of the food's flavors and nutrients. After releasing the pressure, taste the food and adjust the seasonings.
- See specific information about soups, page 9; grains, page 33; meats and poultry, page 51; vegetables, page 101; rice, pages 33, 124-25; beans, pages 124-25; and desserts, page 144.

SOUPS

ABOUT PRESSURE COOKING SOUPS

- Pressure cooking soups with ingredients that tend to foam, such as dried beans and split peas, could cause the valves of the pressure cooker to clog. To avoid this, add 1 tbs. of oil per cup of dried beans when adapting your own recipes.

- If necessary, reduce the liquid content of your original recipe so that it doesn't exceed the maximum fill line of your pressure cooker.

- Another reason for reducing the liquid, especially if the original recipe requires long cooking times without a lid, is that there is very little evaporation during the pressure cooking process.

- Remember that vegetables cook very quickly in a pressure cooker. When adapting recipes, consider adding the vegetables toward the end of the cooking time to ensure tender, not mushy, vegetables.

- Due to the large amount of liquid in soups, the cooker will take a long time to reach high pressure; plan on about 20 minutes.

- Since pressure cooking concentrates flavors, season soups lightly and adjust flavors at the end of the cooking time.

CHICKEN STOCK

Chicken stock is extremely fast to make in a pressure cooker and creates a delicious base for soup and sauce recipes. You can add onion skins for additional flavor and a dark, rich color. If you don't have fresh herbs for the herb bundle (bouquet garni), use powdered herbs tied in a cheesecloth bag. If whole mace is not available, use a piece of whole nutmeg or a pinch of ground nutmeg.

2 lb. chicken parts
1 lb. veal bones
1 gal. cold water
6 carrots, chopped
2 onions, chopped
1 tbs. whole cloves
4 stalks celery, chopped
1 tbs. salt, or to taste
1 tsp. black peppercorns
2 cloves garlic
herb bundle: 1 bunch parsley stalks, 2 bay leaves, 1 sprig fresh rosemary, 1 sprig
    fresh thyme and a piece of whole mace tied together with kitchen string

Place chicken parts and veal bones in the pressure cooker with cold water and bring to a boil. Remove and discard scum that rises to the top of cooker. Once scum has stopped forming, add remaining ingredients. Seal cooker, bring up to high pressure, reduce heat to stabilize pressure and cook for 30 minutes.

Remove cooker from heat, release pressure and strain off solid ingredients. If desired, remove and shred any edible meat from chicken parts and reserve for another use; discard remaining solids. Taste stock and adjust seasonings. Bring stock to room temperature and refrigerate until ready to use. Before reheating, remove and discard solidified fat on top of chilled stock.

FISH STOCK

A good fish stock can make a marvelous soup or a delicious sauce. This recipe takes only minutes to prepare. Use it as a base for fish chowder.

2 tbs. butter
1 cup white mushroom pieces
2 tsp. salt
pinch freshly grated nutmeg
2 tsp. lemon juice
1 small onion, chopped
2 stalks celery, sliced
1 carrot, sliced

1½ cups dry white wine
4 cups water
herb bundle: 1 bay leaf, 1 sprig thyme
    and a few parsley stalks tied together
    with kitchen string
6-10 black peppercorns
2 lb. fish bones from lean fish, such as
    sole, bass, halibut, cod or snapper

Melt butter in the pressure cooker over medium-high heat. Add mushrooms, salt, nutmeg and lemon juice and sauté briskly for 2 to 3 minutes. Stir in remaining ingredients and bring to a boil. Seal cooker, bring up to high pressure, reduce heat to stabilize pressure and cook for 10 minutes.

Remove cooker from heat, release pressure and immediately pour through a strainer; discard solids. Taste stock and adjust seasonings. Bring stock to room temperature and refrigerate until ready to use. Before reheating, remove and discard any solidified fat on top of stock.

LEMON CURRIED PEA SOUP

Because this soup is made from fresh peas instead of dried peas, it has a delicious fresh flavor and cooks in minutes.

1 large onion, sliced
2 carrots, sliced
2 stalks celery, sliced
2 medium potatoes, peeled and sliced
2 cloves garlic, minced
1 tbs. lemon juice
1 tsp. grated fresh lemon peel (zest)

2 tsp. salt
2 tsp. curry powder
1/4 tsp. turmeric
4 cups chicken stock
2 cups fresh or frozen peas
2 cups half-and-half

Add onion, carrots, celery, potatoes, garlic, lemon juice, lemon peel, salt, curry powder, turmeric, 2 cups of the chicken stock and peas to the pressure cooker and bring to a boil. Seal cooker, bring up to high pressure, reduce heat to stabilize pressure and cook for 5 minutes.

Remove cooker from heat and release pressure. Carefully puree hot soup with a food processor or blender until smooth and return to cooker. Add remaining chicken stock and half-and-half. Heat gently uncovered over low heat until just heated through; do not boil. Taste and adjust seasonings.

HEARTY WHITE BEAN SOUP

This substantial winter soup is incredibly tasty. The unpureed soup solids give the soup a little texture. If you wish to make this a vegetarian soup, use vegetable stock and soy sausage.

½ cup butter
3 onions, finely chopped
4 carrots, chopped
6 cloves garlic, minced
¼ cup chopped fresh parsley
2 tsp. dried thyme
2 bay leaves
1 qt. chicken stock or vegetable stock
2½ cups dried white beans, soaked overnight
¼ cup olive oil
2 red bell peppers, chopped
2 green bell peppers, chopped
1 lb. kielbasa or soy sausage, cooked, skinned if desired, diced
salt and pepper to taste

Melt butter in the pressure cooker over medium-high heat and sauté onions and carrots until softened. Add garlic and sauté for 2 minutes. Stir in parsley, thyme, bay leaves and stock. Drain beans, discarding soaking water, and add to cooker. Bring to a boil. Seal cooker, bring up to high pressure, reduce heat to stabilize pressure and cook for 30 minutes.

Remove cooker from heat and carefully release pressure using the *Cold Water Release Method* (see page 5). Test beans. If not tender, repressurize and cook for a few minutes longer.

Strain solids from soup, reserving liquid and about 1 cup of the soup solids. Carefully puree remaining soup solids with a food processor or blender until smooth, adding a little soup liquid if needed to achieve desired texture.

Wipe out pressure cooker, add olive oil and heat over medium-high heat. Sauté chopped bell peppers until tender-crisp. Add pureed soup and reserved soup solids to cooker with diced kielbasa. Seal cooker, bring up to high pressure, reduce heat to stabilize pressure and cook for 15 minutes.

Remove cooker from heat and release pressure. Taste soup and adjust seasonings.

NOTE: Because beans have a tendency to foam when pressure is released, it is especially important that you do not exceed the fill line of pressure cooker.

SPANISH GARBANZO BEAN SOUP

Servings: 8

This traditional soup, which uses both beef and chicken, usually takes several hours to cook. Pressure cooking makes it fast and easy.

3 lb. chicken parts
½ lb. beef stew meat, cut into ½-inch
   cubes
2 lb. beef bones
2½ qt. water
3 leeks, sliced
3-4 carrots, sliced

¼ cup chopped fresh parsley
1 tbs. salt
¼ tsp. nutmeg
large pinch saffron threads
¼ tsp. pepper
1 can (16 oz.) garbanzo beans,
   undrained

Remove skin and bones from chicken and cut chicken meat into bite-sized pieces. Place chicken meat, beef stew meat, chicken bones and beef bones and water in the pressure cooker and bring to a boil. Remove and discard scum that rises to the top. Once scum has stopped forming, seal cooker, bring up to high pressure, reduce heat to stabilize pressure and cook for 20 minutes.

Remove cooker from heat and release pressure. Add remaining ingredients, seal cooker, repressurize and cook for 10 additional minutes.

Remove cooker from heat, release pressure and skim off fat. Taste and adjust seasonings.

LENTIL AND SAUSAGE SOUP WITH CILANTRO

Lentils are a good source of protein. Usually, I find lentils tend to be a little plain, but the addition of spicy sausage and cilantro makes this soup a winner.

6 cups beef stock
3 cups dried red or yellow lentils
3 tbs. olive oil
2 large onions, diced
4 cloves garlic, minced
2 carrots, diced
4 stalks celery, diced

2 tbs. soy sauce
2 tsp. oyster sauce
salt and pepper to taste
2 tbs. cider or balsamic vinegar
1 lb. cooked kielbasa
1/4 cup chopped fresh cilantro

Bring beef stock to a boil in the pressure cooker and stir in lentils. Add oil, onions, garlic, carrots, celery, soy sauce, oyster sauce, salt, pepper and vinegar. Seal cooker, bring up to high pressure, reduce heat to stabilize pressure and cook for 20 minutes.

Remove cooker from heat and release pressure. Cut sausage into bite-sized pieces and add to soup with cilantro. Simmer uncovered for 5 minutes. Taste and adjust seasonings.

VEGETABLE SOUP WITH WINTER PESTO

This Italian favorite is especially good served during the cold months of the year. A dollop of pesto sauce adds tremendous flavor. Pesto is usually made with fresh basil, which is mostly available in the summer. Here, I offer a winter version.

2 cups dried navy and/or pinto beans,
  soaked overnight
3 cans (14½ oz. each) beef broth
2 tbs. olive oil
2 qt. water, plus more if needed
2 tsp. salt
1 small head green cabbage, thinly sliced
4 carrots, sliced
1 can (16 oz.) whole plum tomatoes
2 onions, chopped
¼ cup olive oil

2 stalks celery, chopped
2 zucchini, chopped
1 fresh tomato, chopped
2-3 cloves garlic, minced
1½ tsp. dried basil
1 tbs. tomato paste
¼ cup chopped fresh parsley
1 cup small shell pasta or orzo
pepper and additional salt to taste
Winter Pesto, follows, or purchased
  pesto sauce

Drain beans and discard soaking water. In a 1-quart measuring container, pour beef broth, 2 tbs. oil and enough water to make 1 quart of combined liquid. Pour into the pressure cooker with beans, 2 quarts water and 2 tsp. salt. Bring to a boil. Seal cooker, bring up to high pressure, reduce heat to stabilize pressure and cook for 30 minutes.

Remove cooker from heat and release pressure using the *Cold Water Release Method* (see page 5). Remove 1/2 of the beans, puree with a blender or food processor and return to cooker. Add cabbage, carrots and canned tomatoes. Reseal cooker, bring up to high pressure, reduce heat to stabilize pressure and cook for 10 minutes.

In a skillet, sauté onions in 1/4 cup olive oil over medium heat until softened. Add celery, zucchini, fresh tomato, garlic, basil and tomato paste. Remove cooker from heat and release pressure. Add vegetable mixture, reseal cooker, bring up to high pressure and cook for 7 minutes.

Remove cooker from heat and release pressure. Add parsley and pasta to cooker and simmer uncovered until pasta is tender. Taste and adjust seasonings. Pour soup into bowls and place about 1 tsp. *Winter Pesto* in the center of each bowl.

WINTER PESTO

Makes 1 cup

1/4 cup butter, softened
1/4 cup grated Parmesan cheese
1/2 cup finely chopped fresh parsley
1/4 cup olive oil

1 tsp. dried basil
1/2 tsp. dried marjoram
1/4 cup pine nuts
1 clove garlic, minced

With a food processor or blender, blend butter with Parmesan; add remaining ingredients and process until well mixed.

GARLIC VEGETABLE SOUP

Garlic puree is added to this soup at the last moment along with a sprinkling of Parmesan cheese for a unique twist on a country classic.

3 qt. water
1 leek, diced
1 onion, diced
2 cups green beans
2 cups diced carrots
2 cups diced potatoes, peeled if desired
2 cups diced tomatoes, seeds removed
2 zucchini or yellow summer squash, diced
½ lb. white mushrooms, sliced
1 tbs. salt
pepper to taste
3 cloves garlic, mashed to a paste with a little salt
1 can (6 oz.) tomato paste
¼ cup grated Parmesan cheese, plus more for garnish
¼ cup olive oil
2-3 tbs. chopped fresh basil for garnish

Bring water to a boil in the pressure cooker and add leek, onion, green beans, carrots, potatoes and tomatoes. Seal cooker, bring up to high pressure, reduce heat to stabilize pressure and cook for 10 minutes.

Remove cooker from heat and release pressure. Add zucchini, mushrooms, salt and pepper. Reseal, repressurize and cook for 5 additional minutes.

Mix mashed garlic with tomato paste, ¼ cup Parmesan cheese and olive oil. Remove cooker from heat and release pressure. Add a little hot soup to garlic mixture; stir into soup until well blended and cook uncovered for 5 minutes. Taste and adjust seasonings. Pour into soup bowls and garnish with a little Parmesan and basil.

FRESH TOMATO AND ORANGE SOUP

Here's a refreshing new twist on an old-time favorite. It is delicious served with a dollop of crème fraiche, if it is available, or sour cream. A shortcut version of crème fraiche follows. You can also purchase crème fraiche starter in some supermarkets; follow the directions on the package to make your own. If you feel like a heartier dish, you can add 1 to 2 cups of cooked rice.

3 lb. very ripe fresh tomatoes
1/4 cup butter
1 tbs. olive oil
1 onion, finely minced
3 tbs. flour
herb bundle: 1 bay leaf, few parsley
    stalks, 1 sprig fresh thyme and 1
    sprig fresh marjoram tied together
    with kitchen string

salt and white pepper to taste
4 cups boiling water
1/2 cup orange juice
1 tsp. grated fresh orange peel (zest)
1-2 tsp. sugar, or to taste, optional
1/2 cup crème fraiche, *Mock Crème
    Fraiche*, follows, or sour cream for
    garnish
chopped fresh dill for garnish, optional

Drop tomatoes into boiling water for 1 to 2 minutes, depending on ripeness. Immediately transfer to a bowl of cold water. Remove tomato skins, cut tomatoes in half, squeeze out seeds and chop tomato flesh coarsely.

Heat 1 tbs. of the butter with olive oil in the pressure cooker over medium heat. Add onion and sauté over medium-high heat until lightly browned. Add remaining butter; when melted, add flour, stirring until golden brown. Add chopped tomatoes, stirring constantly. Add herb bundle, salt, white pepper and boiling water. Seal cooker, bring up to high pressure, reduce heat to stabilize pressure and cook for 12 minutes.

Remove cooker from heat and release pressure. Remove and discard herb bundle. Carefully puree hot soup with a food processor or blender. Stir in orange juice, orange peel and sugar, if using. Serve topped with a dollop of crème fraiche, *Mock Crème Fraiche* or sour cream, and/or a sprinkling of dill.

MOCK CRÈME FRAICHE

Makes ½ cup

¼ cup sour cream
¼ cup unsweetened whipped cream

Mix ingredients together in a bowl.

CREAMY CELERY AND POTATO SOUP

This soup is unbelievably fast to prepare, but tastes like it took hours. If desired, garnish with a sprinkling of chopped green onions or chives.

2 tbs. butter
2½ cups diced celery
1 cup diced onion
3 medium potatoes, diced
4 cups water
2½ tsp. salt
⅛ tsp. ground allspice
½ tsp. dried thyme, optional
½ cup heavy cream

Heat butter in the pressure cooker over medium-high heat and sauté celery and onion until softened. Add remaining ingredients, except cream, and bring to a boil. Seal cooker, bring up to high pressure, reduce heat to stabilize pressure and cook for 5 minutes.

Remove cooker from heat and release pressure. Add cream and just heat through over low heat; do not boil. Taste and adjust seasonings.

CREAM OF ASPARAGUS SOUP

When fresh asparagus is in season, asparagus soup should always be on the menu! This is a good starter course for an elegant meal. Traditionally this soup is served with melba toast.

½ cup butter
2 onions, chopped
4 large potatoes, diced
3 lb. asparagus, chopped, tips reserved
   for garnish

1 qt. chicken stock
water, optional
salt and white pepper to taste
2 cups half-and-half
½ tsp. nutmeg

Heat butter in the pressure cooker over medium heat and sauté onions until softened. Stir in potatoes and asparagus and add chicken stock. If necessary, add additional water to cover vegetables. Add salt and white pepper to taste and bring mixture to a boil. Seal cooker, bring up to high pressure, reduce heat to stabilize pressure and cook for 7 minutes.

Remove cooker from heat and release pressure. Carefully pour contents into a blender or food processor, in batches if necessary. Puree hot mixture and return to pressure cooker. Add half-and-half, nutmeg and asparagus tips and reheat gently until tips are cooked; do not boil.

CREAMY PUMPKIN SOUP

When pumpkins are plentiful, pumpkin soup is always popular. Consider serving this soup in a hollowed-out pumpkin shell to impress your guests. Look for small pumpkins for tender, flavorful flesh. For a vegetarian soup, use vegetable stock in place of chicken stock.

3 lb. peeled pumpkin flesh, cubed
1 cup water
¼ cup butter
1 large onion, chopped
4 cups chicken stock
1 tsp. salt
1 bay leaf
½ tsp. curry powder
½ tsp. ground ginger
¼ tsp. nutmeg
white pepper to taste
1 cup half-and-half
dash nutmeg for garnish, optional
sour cream for garnish, optional

Place pumpkin cubes in the steamer basket in the pressure cooker with 1 cup water and bring to a boil. Seal cooker, bring up to high pressure, reduce heat to stabilize pressure and cook for 12 minutes.

Remove cooker from heat and release pressure. Puree cooked pumpkin with a blender or food processor until smooth.

Wipe pressure cooker dry. Melt butter in pressure cooker over medium heat and sauté onion until softened. Add pureed pumpkin to cooker with stock, salt, bay leaf, curry, ginger, nutmeg and pepper and bring to a boil. Seal cooker, bring up to high pressure, reduce heat to stabilize pressure and cook for 5 minutes.

Remove cooker from heat and release pressure. Discard bay leaf and puree ingredients with blender or food processor. Return pureed mixture to cooker, add half-and-half and heat gently to warm through; do not boil. Taste and adjust seasonings. If desired, garnish individual bowls of soup with a sprinkling of nutmeg and a dollop of sour cream.

CORN AND POTATO CHOWDER

This fast, easy chowder is best when made with fresh corn right from the cob, but you can also use frozen corn for an easy version. Add chicken for a heartier soup or use fish stock and add fish pieces for a fish chowder.

½ lb. lean bacon, plus more for
  garnish, optional
2 medium onions, diced
4 cups diced potatoes
4 cups chicken stock

salt and pepper to taste
6 cups corn kernels or frozen corn
1 cup heavy cream
chopped green onions for garnish,
  optional

Dice bacon into small pieces and sauté in the pressure cooker over medium-high heat until crisp. Remove bacon and pour off fat, leaving a small amount in cooker. Add onions to cooker and sauté until golden. Add potatoes, chicken stock, salt and pepper. Bring to a boil. Seal cooker, bring up to high pressure, reduce heat to stabilize pressure and cook for 6 minutes.

Remove cooker from heat and release pressure. Stir in corn. Cook uncovered for 2 to 3 minutes. Add cream and cooked bacon and cook until just heated through; do not boil. Taste and adjust seasonings. Garnish with additional crumbled bacon or green onions if desired.

GREEK LEMON SOUP

This traditional, delicious, refreshing soup serves well as a first course.

2½ qt. chicken stock
1 cup long-grain rice
4 eggs
¼ cup fresh lemon juice
1 tbs. finely chopped fresh parsley

Bring chicken stock to a boil in the pressure cooker and add rice. Seal cooker, bring up to high pressure, reduce heat to stabilize pressure and cook for 6 minutes.

Remove cooker from heat and release pressure. Beat eggs in a bowl until light yellow in color. Whisk lemon juice very slowly into eggs to prevent curdling. Whisk a small amount of hot stock into egg mixture. Whisk stock-egg mixture into rice mixture. Sprinkle with parsley and serve immediately.

MEXICAN TORTILLA SOUP

This unique recipe is fast and full of incredible Mexican flavors. Serve with wedges of lime so your guests can add their own amount of zestiness.

1/4 cup vegetable oil, plus more for
   frying tortillas
2 onions, sliced
5 cloves garlic
1 can (15 oz.) whole tomatoes, drained
3 qt. chicken or beef stock
8-10 corn tortillas

1 tbs. chopped fresh cilantro
salt to taste
chili powder or chopped jalapeño
   pepper to taste, optional
3/4-1 lb. Muenster, Monterey Jack or
   farmer's cheese, shredded
lime wedges

Heat 1/4 cup oil in the pressure cooker over medium-high heat; add onions and garlic and sauté until deep golden brown. Puree mixture with a blender or food processor with tomatoes until smooth; return to cooker. Add stock and bring to a boil. Seal cooker, bring up to high pressure, reduce heat to stabilize pressure and cook for 10 minutes.

Cut tortillas into 1/4-inch wedges. In a skillet, heat frying oil over medium-high heat and fry wedges until crisp; drain on paper towels. Remove cooker from heat and release pressure. Add chopped cilantro and salt. Taste and adjust seasonings, adding chili powder or jalapeños if desired. Divide cheese and tortilla chips equally among bowls and pour hot soup over the top. Serve with lime wedges.

MEATBALL SOUP

This delicious, traditional Mexican soup is fast to fix. It makes a great meal by itself — simply serve with a crisp tossed salad and crusty bread or tortillas. The optional peas will add a little more color and crunch.

2 tbs. vegetable oil
1 onion, minced
2 cloves garlic, minced
1 can (8 oz.) tomato sauce
3 qt. beef stock
2 carrots, diced
¾ lb. ground beef

¾ lb. ground pork
⅓ cup long-grain rice
1 egg, slightly beaten
1 tbs. chopped fresh mint leaves
1½ tsp. salt, or to taste
¼ tsp. pepper
½ cup frozen peas, optional

Heat oil in the pressure cooker over medium heat and sauté onion and garlic until softened. Add tomato sauce, stock and carrots and bring to a boil. In a separate bowl, mix together beef, pork, rice, egg, mint, salt and pepper. Form mixture into 1-inch balls. Drop meatballs into boiling stock mixture. Seal cooker, bring up to high pressure, reduce heat to stabilize pressure and cook for 10 minutes.

Remove cooker from heat and release pressure. Taste and adjust seasonings. If desired, stir in peas and simmer for 1 to 2 minutes.

GRAIN, POTATO AND MEAT SALADS

ABOUT PRESSURE COOKING GRAINS

- When cooking rice and other grains, watch for foaming. Do not exceed the maximum fill line of your pressure cooker.

- Since rice doubles in bulk when cooked, use only half as much uncooked rice as the cooker's capacity will allow. For example, never cook more than 3 cups raw rice in a 6-quart cooker. Brown rice bulks up even more, so start with a little less than half. These amounts will change if there is more than just rice in your recipe.

- Pressure-cooked rice can be slightly stickier than conventionally cooked rice. Use the *Natural Release Method*, page 5, for a better rice texture. For other grains, use the *Cold Water Release Method*, page 5, to avoid foaming.

- When adapting your own rice and grain recipes, avoid clogging the pressure cooker's valves by adding 1 tbs. butter or oil per cup of grains to cooker.

- You can generally use less salt in pressure-cooked grain recipes and there is no need to presoak the grains.

- When adapting your own grain recipes, be aware that the liquid content will vary. Start with the ratios listed here for similar grains and adjust as needed. It's OK to use a little more liquid than you think you will need without exceeding the fill line. Drain off any excess liquid after the grains are cooked.

BULGUR WHEAT SALAD

Bulgur wheat (processed cracked wheat) is a delicious alternative to rice.

2 cups bulgur wheat
4 cups water
1 cup chopped toasted pecans
1 cup dried currants, golden raisins or dark raisins
¼ cup chopped fresh cilantro or tarragon
¼ cup olive oil
2 tbs. grated fresh orange peel (zest)
salt and pepper to taste
orange juice, optional

Bring bulgur and water to a boil in the pressure cooker. Seal cooker, bring up to high pressure, reduce heat to stabilize pressure and cook for 12 minutes.

Remove cooker from heat and release pressure using the *Cold Water Release Method* (see page 5). Test bulgur for doneness by gently fluffing with a fork. If water is still left in cooker, cook uncovered until absorbed. Transfer bulgur to a bowl and cool. Add remaining ingredients, except orange juice, taste and adjust seasonings. Add a small amount of orange juice for a moister salad.

QUINOA SEAFOOD SALAD

Quinoa (pronounced "keen-wah") is an ancient South American grain. It has the highest protein level of any grain and cooks quickly. Look for quinoa in health food stores. You can substitute millet or rice if desired, but the cooking times will increase.

2 cups quinoa
4 cups water
1 cup halved snow peas
4 green onions, cut into shreds
1 cup sliced cucumber
3/4 lb. cooked shrimp and/or crab
1/2 cup chopped fresh cilantro

1/4 cup balsamic vinegar or red wine
   vinegar
2 1/2 tbs. soy sauce
2 1/2 tbs. minced fresh ginger
3 tbs. toasted sesame oil
2 tsp. honey
1/4 tsp. cayenne pepper, or more to taste

Toast quinoa in the pressure cooker over medium heat, stirring until lightly browned. Add water, seal cooker, bring up to high pressure, reduce heat to stabilize pressure and cook for 4 minutes.

Remove cooker from heat and release pressure. Let grain stand for 5 minutes. Transfer quinoa to a bowl and cool. Add snow peas, green onions, cucumber, seafood and cilantro. With a blender or food processor, combine vinegar, soy sauce, ginger, sesame oil, honey and cayenne and process until well blended. Pour over salad and toss well. Taste, adjust seasonings and chill until ready to serve.

RICE AND VEGETABLE MELANGE

Servings: 8

This salad is colorful, versatile and keeps well. Vary the ingredients to your heart's desire for new recipes each time. To blanch peas, plunge them into boiling water for 1 minute. Drain and immediately rinse under cold water.

3 cups long-grain rice
4 cups water
1½-2 cups *Vinaigrette*, follows
1 red bell pepper, cut into strips
1 green or yellow bell pepper, cut into strips
1 medium red onion, diced
6 green onions, finely diced
2 shallots, finely diced
1 cup dried currants or raisins
1 pkg. (10 oz.) frozen peas, thawed and blanched
½ cup sliced Greek olives
¼ cup chopped fresh parsley
½ cup chopped fresh cilantro, dill or basil
salt and pepper to taste

Bring rice and water to a boil in the pressure cooker. Seal cooker, bring up to high pressure, reduce heat to stabilize pressure and cook for 6 minutes.

Remove cooker from heat and release pressure. Mix hot rice with *Vinaigrette*. Cool to room temperature. Add remaining ingredients and toss thoroughly. Taste and adjust seasonings. Serve at room temperature.

VINAIGRETTE

Makes 2 1/4 cups

1 1/2 cups olive oil
3/4 cup balsamic vinegar or red wine vinegar
3 tbs. Dijon mustard
1 tbs. sugar
1 1/2 tsp. salt
1 1/2 tsp. pepper
1/4 cup minced fresh parsley

Mix all ingredients with a food processor or blender until thoroughly blended.

ARTICHOKE RICE SALAD

Flavoring rice with chicken stock intensifies the flavor. This salad has a unique, piquant taste due to the combination of artichoke hearts, green olives and capers. Greek olives add additional flavor and color.

5 cups chicken stock
2 cups long-grain rice
3 jars (6 oz. each) marinated artichoke
   hearts, drained, marinade reserved,
   quartered
5 green onions, sliced
1 red or green bell pepper, diced
1 jar (4 oz.) sliced green olives

1 tbs. capers
3 stalks celery, diced
1/4 cup chopped fresh parsley
1 tsp. curry powder
2 cups mayonnaise
salt and pepper to taste
1/2 cup chopped Greek olives, optional

Bring chicken stock and rice to a boil in the pressure cooker. Seal cooker, bring up to high pressure, reduce heat to stabilize pressure and cook for 6 minutes.

Remove cooker from heat and release pressure. Transfer cooked rice to a large bowl. Add artichokes to rice with green onions, bell pepper, green olives, capers, celery and parsley. Mix curry powder with mayonnaise, salt and pepper and stir gently into rice mixture. If mixture needs to be thinned or needs additional flavor, add a small amount of the reserved artichoke marinade. Stir in Greek olives if using.

SPICY BROWN RICE SALAD

This crunchy, wholesome salad features a spicy mustard dressing. I like to serve this as part of a trio of salads, including a fruit salad and a seafood salad.

2¼ cups water or chicken stock
1 cup brown rice
1 tbs. olive oil, if using water
pinch salt
1 can (8 oz.) chopped water chestnuts
1 jar (2 oz.) chopped pimientos
1 green or yellow bell pepper, chopped
2 cups sliced white mushrooms

½ cup sliced green onions or chives
½ cup chopped fresh parsley
½ cup olive oil
3 tbs. white wine vinegar
1 tbs. soy sauce
2 tbs. spicy mustard
1 tsp. brown sugar
salt and pepper to taste

Bring water to a boil in the pressure cooker. Add rice, oil, if using, and pinch salt. Seal cooker, bring up to high pressure, reduce heat to stabilize pressure and cook for 15 to 18 minutes.

Remove cooker from heat and release pressure using the *Cold Water Release Method* (see page 5). Transfer rice to a bowl and add vegetables and parsley. Mix remaining ingredients with a blender and pour over hot rice mixture. Taste and adjust seasonings. Cool to room temperature before refrigerating. Serve chilled.

CURRIED BROWN RICE SALAD

This can be made into a creamy salad with the addition of mayonnaise and yogurt. The simpler version, without mayonnaise or yogurt, has a more distinct flavor.

2 cups brown rice
2 cans (14½ oz. each) chicken broth
¾ tsp. ground ginger
1 tsp. curry powder
½ tsp. turmeric
½ tsp. salt, or more to taste
pepper to taste
¼ cup olive oil
¼ cup lemon juice
¾ cup chopped red cabbage

½ cup chopped green and/or red bell
  pepper
½ cup golden raisins or dried cranberries
½ cup dried currants
½ cup finely chopped fresh parsley
¼ cup sliced or slivered almonds,
  toasted
⅓ cup mayonnaise, optional
⅓ cup plain yogurt, optional

Place the trivet or steamer basket in the pressure cooker. Add brown rice, chicken broth, ginger, curry, turmeric, salt and pepper and bring to a boil. Seal cooker, bring up to high pressure, reduce heat to stabilize pressure and cook for 17 minutes.

Remove cooker from heat and release pressure using the *Cold Water Release Method* (see page 5). Transfer rice mixture to a serving bowl. Mix together oil and lemon juice and stir into rice mixture. Refrigerate until well chilled.

Stir cabbage, bell pepper, raisins, currants, parsley and almonds into cold rice. Taste and adjust seasonings. For a creamy salad, stir in mayonnaise and yogurt. Chill until ready to serve.

FRUITED WILD RICE SALAD

Wild rice adds a delightful chewy texture to a rice salad. This is great as an accompaniment to pork and ham dishes.

3 cups chicken stock or water
¾ cup wild rice
½ cup dark raisins
½ cup golden raisins
½ cup chopped dried apricots
boiling water
¾ cup long-grain rice
1 cup chopped toasted almonds or walnuts
1 cup red and/or green seedless grapes
¾ cup sliced green onions
¼ cup chopped fresh parsley
½ cup olive oil
juice and grated peel (zest) of 2 lemons
2 tbs. honey
1 tbs. chopped fresh mint
salt and pepper to taste

Bring 1½ cups of the chicken stock to a boil in the pressure cooker and add wild rice. Seal cooker, bring up to high pressure, reduce heat to stabilize pressure and cook for 15 minutes. While wild rice is cooking, place raisins and apricots in a bowl and cover with boiling water to plump.

Remove cooker from heat and release pressure. Transfer wild rice to a bowl and cool. Bring remaining 1½ cups chicken stock to a boil in pressure cooker and add long-grain rice. Seal cooker, bring up to high pressure, reduce heat to stabilize pressure and cook for 6 minutes.

Remove cooker from heat and release pressure. Transfer rice to bowl with wild rice. Mix walnuts, grapes, plumped raisins and apricots and green onions with rice. Chill.

In a blender container, combine parsley, olive oil, lemon juice and zest, honey, mint, salt and pepper and blend until well mixed. Add dressing to rice and toss thoroughly. Chill until ready to serve.

RED POTATO SALAD

You can vary the herbs and dressings to create endless varieties of potato salad. For better flavor, add the dressing while the potatoes are still warm.

$2\frac{1}{2}$ lb. small red potatoes
1 cup water
$\frac{1}{4}$ cup wine vinegar
1 tbs. Dijon mustard
1 tsp. salt
pepper to taste
1 cup olive oil
2 green onions, sliced
$\frac{1}{4}$ cup chopped fresh dill, basil or cilantro, loosely packed
salt and pepper to taste
1 cup sour cream

Wash potatoes, but do not peel. Leave small potatoes whole and cut larger ones in half. Place potatoes in the steamer basket in the pressure cooker. Add water and bring to a boil. Seal cooker, bring up to high pressure, reduce heat to stabilize pressure and cook for 7 to 9 minutes.

Place vinegar, mustard, salt and pepper in a blender container or food processor workbowl. With machine running, slowly add oil in a thin stream until all oil is well incorporated.

Remove cooker from heat and release pressure. Cut warm potatoes in half, add dressing and mix well. Gently stir in onions, dill, salt, pepper and sour cream. Let stand for at least 30 minutes before serving.

MANGO CHUTNEY CHICKEN SALAD

This recipe has a slightly spicy, tropical flavor. One trick to good chicken salad is flavoring the chicken during the initial cooking stage.

1 chicken, about 3-3½ lb., cut into
  serving pieces and skinned
2 cups water or chicken stock
1 bay leaf
1 onion, quartered
1 tsp. salt
2 stalks celery, coarsely chopped
1 tsp. black peppercorns
1 carrot, coarsely chopped
handful parsley stalks

1 lb. celery, diced
1 bunch green onions, sliced
1 cup slivered almonds, toasted
1 cup pineapple tidbits, drained
1 cup cubed fresh mango
2¼ cups mayonnaise
½ cup mango chutney
1 tbs. lemon juice
1 tsp. curry powder
½ tsp. salt, or more to taste

Place chicken pieces, water, bay leaf, onion, salt, celery, peppercorns, carrot and parsley stalks in the pressure cooker on the trivet and bring to a boil. Seal cooker, bring up to high pressure, reduce heat to stabilize pressure and cook for 15 minutes.

Remove cooker from heat and release pressure. Remove chicken parts. If desired, strain liquid and use as chicken stock; discard remaining solids.

When chicken is cool, remove bones, cut chicken meat into cubes and place in a bowl. Add diced celery, green onions, almonds, pineapple and mango. Mix mayonnaise, chutney, lemon juice, curry powder and salt in a separate bowl. Mix enough dressing with chicken to moisten. Taste and adjust seasonings.

TROPICAL CHICKEN PAPAYA SALAD

Servings: 6

Serve this unique, flavorful salad with banana or date bread. For a change, try mango instead of papaya.

6 chicken breast halves
1 cup water
1 cup chopped celery
½ cup chopped onion
½ tsp. salt
½ tsp. black peppercorns
salad greens
3 avocados, peeled and sliced
3 ripe papayas, peeled, seeded and sliced

½ cup orange juice
grated peel (zest) of 1 orange
2 tbs. minced fresh tarragon
¼ cup sour cream
¾ cup vegetable oil
3 tbs. balsamic vinegar
1 clove garlic, minced
salt and pepper to taste

Place chicken breasts, water, celery, onion, salt and peppercorns in the pressure cooker on the trivet and bring to a boil. Seal cooker, bring up to high pressure, reduce heat to stabilize pressure and cook for 10 minutes.

Remove cooker from heat and release pressure. Cool chicken, remove skin and bones and cut meat into slivers. Arrange salad greens on individual plates. Evenly distribute chicken meat, avocado and papaya among plates. Blend remaining ingredients with a blender or food processor and drizzle over salads.

TACO SALAD

If you like your Mexican food hot, add more jalapeño peppers or a dash of Tabasco Sauce to the beef recipe.

8 cups shredded lettuce
½ recipe *Mexican Shredded Beef*, page 65
4 cups shredded cheddar, Monterey Jack and/or Muenster cheese
1 cup chopped black olives
4 green onions, chopped
2-3 cups chopped fresh tomatoes
tortilla chips for garnish
sour cream or guacamole for garnish, optional
salad dressing for garnish, optional

Arrange a bed of lettuce on each of 8 dinner plates. Divide shredded beef among plates and sprinkle with cheddar cheese, olives, green onions and fresh tomatoes. Place tortilla chips around the outside edges and serve with garnishes of choice.

BEEF AND LAMB ENTRÉES

ABOUT PRESSURE COOKING MEATS AND POULTRY

- When adapting recipes for braised meats, allow 20 minutes of cooking time per pound of meat. Use 1 cup liquid for the first pound and $\frac{1}{2}$ cup for each additional pound.

- When in doubt about the proper cooking time for meats or poultry, undercook the food rather than take a chance of overcooking it. Taste the food, and if necessary, reseal and repressurize the pressure cooker, cooking for a few more minutes.

- Watch for scorching if browning the meats ahead of time. Using the trivet and a small amount of liquid after browning will help.

- For steam-roasting poultry, brown it first in oil. Add the trivet and 1 cup water to the pressure cooker. Plan for 5 minutes of cooking time per pound of unstuffed poultry, and 8 minutes per pound for stuffed poultry (weight of poultry before stuffing).

- Removing the skin from the chicken parts before pressure cooking makes a better finished dish. It also reduces the fat content.

BARBECUE COUNTRY RIBS

Boiling ribs in water flavored with aromatic vegetables, seasonings and vinegar reduces greasiness and adds a lot of flavor.

4 lb. country-style beef ribs	2 carrots, coarsely chopped
water	2 stalks celery, chopped
1 tbs. salt	2 tbs. cider vinegar
1 tbs. black peppercorns	2 bay leaves
1 onion, with skin, coarsely chopped	bottled barbecue sauce

Trim excessive fat from ribs. Fill the pressure cooker halfway with water, but do not exceed the fill line. Place the steamer basket in pressure cooker and add ribs and remaining ingredients, except barbecue sauce. Bring water to a boil. Seal cooker, bring up to high pressure, reduce heat to stabilize pressure and cook for 20 minutes.

Heat broiler. Remove cooker from heat and release pressure. Immediately remove cooked ribs and discard remaining ingredients. Place ribs on a baking sheet fitted with a broiler rack. Brush ribs liberally with barbecue sauce and place under broiler until warmed and browned. Serve immediately.

ITALIAN MEAT SAUCE

Makes: 2 quarts

This favorite meat sauce recipe cooks quickly in the pressure cooker. Use smoked Italian sausage for a unique flavor. If fresh basil is available, chop some and stir in a handful just before serving. Serve over hot cooked pasta.

1/4 cup olive oil
1 large onion, chopped
3 cloves garlic, minced
1 1/2 lb. ground beef chuck
1/2 lb. ground pork or Italian sausage
1-2 lb. mixed meats, such as steaks, ribs, chops and/or beef bones

1/2 cup dry red wine
2 cans (28 oz. each) whole plum tomatoes
2 cans (6 oz. each) tomato paste
1 tsp. dried oregano
1/2 tsp. dried basil
salt and pepper to taste

Heat oil in the pressure cooker over medium-high heat and sauté onion and garlic until softened. Add meats and cook until no red remains. Add wine and cook for several minutes to evaporate alcohol. Coarsely mash tomatoes with a knife and add to cooker with remaining ingredients. Bring to a boil, scraping the bottom of cooker very well. Seal cooker, bring up to high pressure, reduce heat to stabilize pressure and cook for 10 minutes.

Remove cooker from heat and release pressure. Taste and adjust seasonings. Remove bones, shred meat into bite-sized pieces, return meat to sauce and discard bones.

HUNGARIAN GOULASH

*Here is another long-cooking dish that can be made in about 30 minutes, which makes it "do-able" for harried lifestyles. Instead of adding sour cream to the stew, I prefer to serve it over **Sour Cream Noodles**. Paprika is an important part of this recipe, so use a fresh, good-quality brand.*

¼ cup olive oil
3 onions, thinly sliced
4 lb. beef stew meat, cut into 1-inch cubes
2 tbs. flour
2 tsp. salt
2 tsp. caraway seeds
¼ cup paprika
1 tsp. dried marjoram
2 tsp. red wine vinegar
2 cups beef stock
1 cup dry red wine
2 green bell peppers, chopped

Heat oil in a skillet over medium heat and sauté onions until softened. Coat meat with flour, add to skillet and sauté until meat is browned on all sides. Place the trivet in the pressure cooker, add meat mixture and remaining ingredients, except green peppers, and bring to a boil. Seal cooker, bring up to high pressure, reduce heat to stabilize pressure and cook for 20 minutes.

Remove cooker from heat and release pressure. Add green peppers, reseal, repressurize and cook for 10 additional minutes.

Remove cooker from heat and release pressure. Taste and adjust seasonings. Serve with or on top of *Sour Cream Noodles*.

SOUR CREAM NOODLES

Servings: 8-10

1½ lb. small shell, bow-tie or fettuccine pasta
⅓ cup butter, melted
2 cups sour cream
salt to taste
water, optional

Cook pasta according to package directions until slightly firm to the bite, *al dente*. Drain pasta well and toss with melted butter. Stir in sour cream and salt. Add a little water if noodles seem too dry.

BEEF AND GARLIC STEW PROVENÇAL

Servings: 8

This traditional French stew is heavily flavored with garlic and wine. Ideally it should be prepared a day in advance, so the flavors can fully penetrate the meat. I like to serve this with a green salad, French bread and a potato or rice side dish. Be sure to use a good, full-bodied red wine.

4 lb. beef brisket, fat trimmed
1 lb. lean bacon, diced
salt and pepper to taste
4 large onions, cut into quarters
2 heads garlic, separated into cloves and peeled
1 tbs. grated fresh orange peel (zest)
2 bay leaves
1 tsp. dried thyme
dry red wine

Cut meat into large cubes, about 1½ inches. Cook bacon in a skillet over medium-high heat until fat is released; remove bacon and set aside. Cook beef cubes in bacon fat until browned on all sides, in batches if necessary. Sprinkle with salt and pepper. Stir in onion quarters and cooked bacon. Place the trivet in the pressure cooker and add browned meat mixture with garlic cloves. Add orange peel, bay leaves, thyme and enough wine to barely cover contents of pot. Seal cooker, bring up to high pressure, reduce heat to stabilize pressure and cook for 1 hour.

Remove cooker from heat and release pressure. Test meat for tenderness. If meat is not very tender, repressurize and cook for 15 additional minutes. Cool stew to room temperature, remove bay leaves and refrigerate overnight, if possible. Skim off any solidified fat on the surface of stew. Bring stew to a boil before serving.

BEEF BOURGUIGNONNE

This is a deep, rich, wine-flavored stew that goes well on buttered noodles, **Sour Cream Noodles**, *page 55, or steamed rice. The French traditionally serve a green salad after the meal to refresh the palate. For added flavor and color, add carrot and celery chunks with the onions.*

2 tbs. olive oil
4 lb. beef stew meat, cubed
1 tbs. sugar
1 tbs. red wine vinegar
1½ cups dry red wine
1½ cups beef stock
1½ tsp. salt
pepper to taste
2 tbs. olive oil
2 large onions, sliced
12 small boiling onions, peeled
water
¼ cup butter
2½ lb. white mushrooms, sliced
1 tsp. lemon juice

Heat 2 tbs. oil in a skillet over medium-high heat and brown meat on all sides. Push meat to one side of skillet and sprinkle sugar in skillet directly over heat. When sugar starts to caramelize, add vinegar and stir to blend. Add wine, beef stock, salt and pepper.

In the pressure cooker, heat 2 tbs. oil over medium heat and sauté sliced onions until softened. Add beef mixture. Seal cooker, bring up to high pressure, reduce heat to stabilize pressure and cook for 40 minutes.

In a saucepan, cover small whole onions with water and boil until tender, about 14 minutes; drain. In the same skillet in which you cooked beef, heat butter over medium-high heat and sauté mushrooms with lemon juice until softened. Add whole onions to skillet with mushrooms and sauté until onions are glazed.

Remove cooker from heat and release pressure. Add mushrooms and onions. Repressurize and cook for 5 additional minutes. Serve immediately.

CORNED BEEF AND CABBAGE

Servings: 6-8

In our family, St. Patrick's Day is always celebrated by eating corned beef, boiled vegetables and, of course, Irish soda bread. This is my mother's recipe, which has been adapted to the pressure cooker. For a change of pace, you can add cubed parsnips or rutabagas.

4 lb. pickled corned beef, in 2 equal pieces
water
12 small red or white potatoes, peeled
12 carrots, cut in half
12 small boiling onions, peeled
1½ heads green cabbage, cut into wedges
purchased horseradish sauce
mustard

Place the trivet in the pressure cooker. Add corned beef pieces, including all pickling spices. Add enough water to cover meat, but do not to exceed the fill line. Bring water to a boil. Seal cooker, bring up to high pressure, reduce heat to stabilize pressure and cook for 1 hour.

Remove cooker from heat and release pressure using the *Cold Water Release Method* (see page 5). Remove meat and set aside. Place potatoes, carrots and onions in cooking liquid and bring to a boil. Seal cooker, bring up to high pressure, reduce heat to stabilize pressure and cook for 2 to 3 minutes.

Remove cooker from heat and release pressure. Add cabbage wedges. Reseal, repressurize and cook for 2 to 3 additional minutes. Test vegetables for doneness. If vegetables are not done, simmer uncovered until tender. Slice meat across the grain, place on a serving platter and surround with vegetables. Accompany with horseradish sauce and mustard.

MOLASSES AND CIDER POT ROAST

Apple cider and molasses make this roast unique. Remember: this has to marinate for 24 hours; do the advance preparation the night before you plan to cook it.

2 cups apple cider
2 tbs. light molasses
2 tsp. salt
8 whole allspice berries
1/2 tsp. black peppercorns
2 cloves garlic, minced
1/2 tsp. ground ginger
6 lb. beef chuck roast
4 large onions, quartered
4 stalks celery, coarsely chopped
1/4 cup butter
3 tbs. arrowroot or cornstarch
3 tbs. water

Mix apple cider, molasses, salt, allspice, peppercorns, garlic and ginger together. Place beef, onions and celery in a large dish and pour apple cider mixture over meat and vegetables. Cover, refrigerate and marinate for 24 hours.

Remove meat from marinade and wipe dry. Heat butter in a skillet over medium-high heat and brown pot roast very well on all sides. Place the trivet in the pressure cooker and place meat on top. Pour in marinade and vegetables and bring to a boil. Seal cooker, bring up to high pressure, reduce heat to stabilize pressure and cook for 45 minutes to 1 hour.

Remove cooker from heat and release pressure. Strain out meat and vegetables, reserving juices. Return strained juices to cooker and bring to a boil. Mix arrowroot with water and add to heated juices, stirring until thickened. Taste and adjust seasonings. Serve sliced meat with thickened juices.

POT ROAST EXTRAORDINAIRE

This roast is made special by ham strips and garlic cloves, which are inserted into the meat for added flavor.

6 lb. beef chuck roast
¾ lb. ham, cut into 1-x-½-inch strips
4 cloves garlic, cut into small pieces
salt and pepper to taste
¼ cup vegetable oil
1 onion, chopped

1 can (16 oz.) whole plum tomatoes
1 cup dry white wine
1 bay leaf
¼-½ tsp. dried thyme
1 can (4 oz.) button mushrooms
  drained

With the sharp point of a knife, make several pockets in meat and insert ham and garlic pieces. Rub roast with salt and pepper. Heat oil in a skillet over medium-high heat and brown roast on all sides. Place the trivet in the pressure cooker, set browned roast on top and add remaining ingredients, except mushrooms. Bring to a boil. Seal cooker, bring up to high pressure, reduce heat to stabilize pressure and cook for 40 minutes.

Remove cooker from heat and release pressure. Stir in mushrooms and remove bay leaf. Taste and adjust seasonings.

MEXICAN SHREDDED BEEF

*This is great meat for tacos, enchiladas, tamales, burritos, omelets and many other Mexican-style dishes, such as **Taco Salad**, page 49.*

5 lb. beef chuck roast or stew meat
vegetable oil
1 onion, diced
1 red bell pepper, diced
1 green bell pepper, diced
1 jalapeño pepper, seeded and finely
   minced
1/2 bunch fresh cilantro, finely chopped

3 medium tomatoes, seeded and cut
   into wedges
1 1/2 tbs. ground cumin
3-4 tsp. salt, or to taste
2-3 tsp. pepper, or to taste
water

Remove any visible fat from meat. Heat enough oil to cover the bottom of the pressure cooker over medium-high heat. Brown meat on all sides with onion. Add remaining ingredients and stir well, scraping up all browned meat bits. Add enough water to cover meat and bring to a boil. Seal cooker, bring up to high pressure, reduce heat to stabilize pressure and cook for 1 hour.

Remove cooker from heat and release pressure. Test meat for tenderness. If it does not shred easily, repressurize and cook for 15 additional minutes. Pull meat into shreds with fingers. Taste and adjust seasonings.

CREAMY BEEF AND NOODLE BAKE

Layers of noodles, meat and creamy cheese make this a luscious casserole. If you are cutting down on beef, substitute ground turkey.

1 pkg. (8 oz.) egg noodles
2 lb. lean ground beef
1 can (16 oz.) tomato sauce
salt and pepper to taste
1 cup cottage cheese
8 oz. cream cheese, softened

1 cup sour cream
2/3 cup chopped green onions
1-2 tbs. chopped red or green bell
  pepper
1/2-3/4 cup grated Parmesan cheese
1 cup water

Cook noodles according to package directions and set aside to cool. In a skillet, brown ground beef. Stir in tomato sauce and season with salt and pepper. In a bowl, mix together cottage cheese, cream cheese, sour cream, green onions and bell pepper. Grease a casserole dish that fits in the pressure cooker. Layer 1/2 of the noodles in dish and cover with cheese mixture. Layer remaining noodles on top and cover with tomato beef sauce. Sprinkle with Parmesan. Cover entire dish with aluminum foil, sealing the edges well. Place dish on the trivet in cooker and add water. Seal cooker, bring up to high pressure, reduce heat to stabilize pressure, and cook for 10 minutes.

Heat broiler. Remove cooker from heat and release pressure. Remove foil and place dish under broiler until cheese is nicely browned.

CREAMY BEEF CASSEROLE WITH WINE AND MUSHROOMS

This dish is excellent served over hot buttered noodles or rice.

2 tbs. butter
2 tbs. vegetable oil
2 large onions, diced
¾ lb. white mushrooms, sliced
2 lb. top round steak, sliced into thin
   2-inch strips
1 cup beef stock

1 cup dry red wine
1 tsp. dried basil
⅛ tsp. nutmeg
salt and pepper to taste
1½ cups water
2 cups sour cream
1 tbs. prepared horseradish

Heat butter and oil in a skillet over medium-high heat and sauté onions and mushrooms until softened. Remove onion mixture and set aside. Quickly brown meat in skillet and set aside. Grease a casserole dish that fits in the pressure cooker. Add remaining ingredients, except sour cream and horseradish, to dish. Cover entire dish with aluminum foil, sealing the edges well. Place on the trivet in cooker and add water. Seal cooker, bring up to high pressure, reduce heat to stabilize pressure and cook for 40 minutes.

Remove cooker from heat and release pressure. Remove foil and stir in sour cream and horseradish just before serving.

TENDER MEAT LOAF

Servings: 6

There are endless varieties of meat loaf recipes, but what makes this special is the addition of sour cream. Use light sour cream if you wish to reduce the fat content. For extra color, add red bell pepper.

1½ lb. lean ground beef
½ cup minced onion
1½ cups fresh breadcrumbs
2 eggs
1½ tsp. Worcestershire sauce
1¼ tsp. dry mustard

1¼ tsp. salt
½ tsp. pepper
½ cup sour cream
¼ cup diced red bell pepper, optional
1½ cups water

Mix all ingredients, except water, in a bowl until well combined. In a small skillet, sauté about 2 tbs. of the mixture until cooked through; taste and adjust seasonings in remaining mixture. Press remaining mixture into a deep casserole dish that fits in the pressure cooker. Wrap entire dish with aluminum foil, sealing the edges well. Place the trivet in pressure cooker, add water and place meat loaf on trivet. Bring water to a boil. Seal cooker, bring up to high pressure, reduce heat to stabilize pressure and cook for 35 minutes.

Heat broiler if desired. Remove cooker from heat and release pressure. Remove foil and place dish under broiler to brown if desired. Drain off excess fat. Let meat loaf stand for 10 minutes before slicing.

VARIATIONS

ITALIAN MEAT LOAF: Substitute ½ cup tomato sauce for sour cream. Omit mustard and Worcestershire and add ¼ cup minced fresh parsley, ½ tsp. dried oregano and 1 tsp. dried basil. If desired, spread top with ketchup or additional tomato sauce.

CHEESY MEAT LOAF: Omit Worcestershire sauce, increase dry mustard to 1½ tsp. and add ½-¾ cup grated cheese.

MIXED MEAT LOAF: For a unique flavor, use a combination of mixed ground meats. I suggest: ½ lb. ground beef or ground chuck, ½ lb. ground veal or ground venison and ½ lb. ground pork or bulk sausage. If desired, substitute ground turkey for part of the meat to reduce the fat content. Add 1 tsp. minced garlic and, if desired, replace ¼ cup of the sour cream with ¼ cup dry red wine.

CORN TAMALE PIE

Tamale pie is delicious, but it usually takes a long time to cook. Pressure cooking cuts the time down considerably, so now you can enjoy this dish even during the busy work week.

2 tbs. corn oil
1 large onion, diced
1 lb. ground beef, prefer chili grind
1 tbs. chili powder
1/2 tsp. dried oregano
1 clove garlic, minced
1/2 tsp. ground cumin
1/2 tsp. salt
1/4 tsp. pepper

1 cup corn kernels
2 cups crushed tomatoes
2 tbs. ketchup
1/2 cup sliced black olives
Cornmeal Mush, follows
1/3 cup grated cheddar, Monterey Jack
    or other cheese
1 cup water

Heat oil in the pressure cooker over medium-high heat. Add onion and ground beef and sauté until onion is softened. Add seasonings, corn, tomatoes, ketchup and olives and bring to a boil. Stir well to remove small bits of meat stuck on the bottom. Seal cooker, bring up to high pressure, reduce heat to stabilize pressure and cook for 10 minutes.

Grease a 1½-quart casserole dish that fits in cooker. Spread ⅔ of the prepared *Cornmeal Mush* in dish, add meat mixture and cover with remaining ⅓ *Cornmeal Mush*. Sprinkle with grated cheese. Cover entire dish with aluminum foil, sealing the edges well. Place dish in pressure cooker on the trivet or in the steamer basket. Pour water in cooker and bring to a boil. Seal cooker, bring up to high pressure, reduce heat to stabilize pressure and cook for 10 minutes.

Heat broiler. Remove cooker from heat and release pressure. Remove foil and place casserole under broiler for a few minutes to brown cheese.

CORNMEAL MUSH

Makes: 2 cups

1½ cups water
½ cup cornmeal
½ cup cold water

½ tsp. salt
1½ tsp. chili powder

Bring 1½ cups water to a boil in a saucepan. Mix cornmeal and cold water together and stir into boiling water. Add salt and chili powder and cook, stirring occasionally, for 10 minutes, until thickened.

HUNGARIAN CABBAGE ROLLS

*Stuffed cabbage rolls are standard fare at our house. Generally we serve them without a sauce. Here I've added and optional recipe for **Quick Tomato Sauce**. For another variation, cover the bottom of the steamer basket with a layer of sauerkraut and place the cabbage rolls on top to cook.*

1 large head green cabbage, core
   removed
water
1 cup shredded green cabbage
¾ cup long-grain rice
½ cup diced onion
¼ cup diced celery

¼ cup diced carrot
1 lb. ground beef
¾ tsp. salt
½ tsp. pepper
1 cup water
Quick Tomato Sauce, follows, optional

Place cabbage head in the pressure cooker. Cover with water, bring to a boil and boil uncovered for 5 minutes. Carefully remove outer leaves of cabbage and boil for a few additional minutes, until pliable. Separate remaining leaves and set aside. Mix remaining ingredients, except water and sauce, in a bowl. Cut a small V-shaped portion from the tough part of cabbage stems on each leaf to make them easier to roll.

Cup a cabbage leaf in your hand and place about 1/4-1/2 cup filling inside. Loosely wrap leaves around filling to allow rice to expand and secure with a toothpick. Repeat until all filling and/or leaves have been used. Place cabbage rolls in steamer basket and set in pressure cooker. Pour in 1 cup water, seal cooker, bring up to high pressure, reduce heat to stabilize pressure and cook for 30 minutes.

Remove cooker from heat and release pressure. Remove toothpicks from cabbage rolls and serve plain or with *Quick Tomato Sauce*.

QUICK TOMATO SAUCE

Makes: 3 cups

2 cups crushed tomatoes
2 tbs. balsamic vinegar
1 cup sour cream
salt and pepper to taste
1 tsp. dried basil, optional

Heat crushed tomatoes and vinegar in a saucepan. Add sour cream, salt, pepper and basil. Heat gently, stirring until smooth. Pour over cabbage rolls.

GARLIC LAMB STEW

For a good lamb stew, start with a good lamb or veal stock. Pressure cooking makes stocks easily, so take the little extra time to make it special. Herbes de Provence is a French spice blend that can be found in specialty food stores. If you can't find it, mix dried thyme, oregano, marjoram, savory and crumbled bay leaves to taste.

4-5 lb. lamb shoulder
¼ cup olive oil
4 heads garlic, separated into cloves,
   unpeeled
1 cup dry white wine

2 cups *Lamb Stock*, follows, or veal stock
2½ tbs. herbes de Provence
salt and pepper to taste
¼ cup butter, optional
2 tbs. minced fresh parsley for garnish

Cut lamb from shoulder bone and use bone for stock if desired. Remove excessive fat and gristle from lamb and cut into large chunks. Heat oil in the pressure cooker over medium-high heat and brown lamb pieces on all sides. Add garlic cloves and sauté for several minutes. Add wine, stock, herbs, salt and pepper and bring to a boil. Seal cooker, bring up to high pressure, reduce heat to stabilize pressure and cook for 45 minutes.

Remove cooker from heat and release pressure. Test meat: it should be tender, but not stringy. If not tender enough, reseal, repressurize and cook for 15 additional minutes. Remove meat from sauce and keep warm. Press garlic cloves to extract pulp and add to sauce; discard peels. Stir in butter, if using. Taste and adjust seasonings. Serve sauce over lamb chunks and garnish with parsley.

LAMB STOCK

Makes: about 1½ quarts

2 tbs. vegetable oil
½ onion, chopped
bone from lamb shoulder, or 2 lb. veal
    bones
2 chicken bouillon cubes
1 carrot, chopped

2 stalks celery, chopped
herb bundle: 1 bay leaf, few fresh
    parsley stalks and 1 sprig fresh thyme,
    tied together with kitchen string
½ tsp. black peppercorns
water

Heat oil in the pressure cooker over medium heat and sauté onion until softened. Add remaining ingredients, barely covering with water. Bring to a boil and skim any foam that rises to surface. When foam stops forming, seal cooker, bring up to high pressure, reduce heat to stabilize pressure and cook for 10 minutes.

Remove cooker from heat and release pressure. Strain stock, discard solids and skim fat.

LAMB COUSCOUS

Pressure cooking makes this once time-consuming dish a snap. You can substitute beef for the lamb if you choose.

2 tbs. vegetable oil
1½ lb. lamb stew meat, cubed
1 onion, diced
4 tomatoes, skinned, seeded and chopped
3 cloves garlic, minced
1 tsp. ground ginger
1 tsp. crushed fennel seeds, optional
1 tsp. hot pepper sauce
1 tsp. turmeric
1½ cups water or beef stock
2-3 carrots, cut into large chunks
1 large zucchini, cut into large chunks
6 red potatoes, halved if large
salt to taste
1 pkg. (16 oz.) couscous

Heat oil in a skillet over medium-high heat and brown meat on all sides with onion. Transfer mixture to the pressure cooker and add tomatoes, garlic, ginger, fennel, hot pepper sauce, turmeric and water. Bring to a boil. Seal cooker, bring up to high pressure, reduce heat to stabilize pressure and cook for 25 minutes.

Cook couscous according to package directions and keep warm.

Remove cooker from heat and release pressure. Add vegetables, reseal, repressurize and cook for 5 additional minutes. Taste and adjust seasonings. Serve over cooked couscous.

MORE ENTRÉES

MEATLESS TOMATO SAUCE

This is a quick and simple vegetarian tomato sauce that is excellent over pasta or steamed spaghetti squash.

1/4 cup olive oil
1 medium onion, chopped
2 cloves garlic, minced
2 cans (28 oz. each) whole plum
  tomatoes, coarsely chopped
1 can (6 oz.) tomato paste

1/4 cup minced fresh parsley
1-2 tbs. chopped fresh basil, or 1-2 tsp.
  dried
1 1/2 tsp. dried oregano
1/2 cup dry red wine
salt and pepper to taste

Heat oil in the pressure cooker over medium heat and sauté onion until softened; add garlic and sauté for 1 minute. Add tomatoes and remaining ingredients and bring to a boil, stirring constantly. Seal cooker, bring up to high pressure, reduce heat to stabilize pressure and cook for 10 minutes.

Remove cooker from heat and release pressure. Taste and adjust seasonings.

MIXED BEAN VEGETARIAN CHILI

A favorite trick for making a tasty chili is to use several kinds of beans, which adds additional flavor and color. I like to serve this with hot cornbread.

1 red bell pepper
1 green bell pepper
3 tbs. vegetable oil
2 medium onions, chopped
1 jalapeño pepper, seeded and finely minced,
    or more to taste, optional
1 can (4 oz.) chopped green chiles
4 cloves garlic, minced
leaves from 1 bunch fresh parsley, chopped
3 cans (15 oz. each) pinto, kidney, navy
    and/or black beans, rinsed and drained
1 can (28 oz.) crushed tomatoes
4 tsp. salt
1 tsp. ground cumin
1 tsp. dried oregano
2 tbs. chili powder
2 cups water
2 tbs. chopped fresh cilantro

Cut bell peppers into roughly ½-inch squares. Heat oil in the pressure cooker over medium heat and sauté onions until softened. Add bell peppers, jalapeño, green chiles, garlic, chopped parsley and beans. Coarsely chop tomatoes and add to mixture with salt, cumin, oregano, chili powder and water. Seal cooker, bring up to high pressure, reduce heat to stabilize pressure and cook for 15 minutes.

Remove cooker from heat and release pressure. Add chopped cilantro, taste and adjust seasonings.

VARIATION: MEATY THREE-BEAN CHILI

Brown 1 lb. ground beef or turkey and add to cooked chili.

NOTE: These recipes make large batches of chili. Do not exceed your pressure cooker's capacity; reduce the recipes if necessary.

RASPBERRY CHICKEN

This is an absolutely delicious chicken recipe, but depending on the type of jam used, it can take on a very dark color. I enhance the appearance by garnishing with fine shreds of orange peel. If available, garnish with a sprinkling of fresh raspberries.

½ cup fruity red wine
½ cup raspberry vinegar or red wine
   vinegar
½-1 cup raspberry jam
2 tbs. soy sauce
2-3 tbs. honey
1 tsp. Dijon mustard

1 clove garlic, minced
1 chicken, 3-3½ lb., cut into serving
   pieces and skinned
slivered fresh orange peel (zest) for
   garnish
fresh raspberries for garnish, optional

In a bowl, combine wine, vinegar, jam, soy sauce, honey, mustard and garlic and stir until well mixed. Taste and adjust sweetness. Pour mixture over chicken and marinate for at least 4 hours, but preferably overnight, in the refrigerator.

Place chicken and marinade in the pressure cooker and bring to a boil. Seal cooker, bring up to high pressure, reduce heat to stabilize pressure and cook for 12 minutes.

Remove cooker from heat and release pressure. Remove chicken, leaving marinade in cooker. Boil marinade uncovered until it reaches desired thickness. Pour over chicken and garnish with thinly sliced orange peel and fresh raspberries, if using.

PARMESAN PORTOBELLO PASTA

ep Time: 20 minutes   Cook Time: 10 minutes

lb. bow-tie pasta	1 medium zucchini, sliced ½ inch thick
tbsp. olive oil	
lb. portobello mushrooms, cut into bite-size pieces	1 tbsp. minced garlic
	1 tbsp. red wine vinegar
red bell pepper, seeded and cut into ½-inch pieces	½ cup grated Parmesan cheese

Cook pasta according to package directions until tender but firm. Drain, reserving ½ cup pasta water.

Meanwhile, in large nonstick skillet heat oil over medium heat. Add mushrooms, bell pepper, zucchini and garlic; cook 5 to 7 minutes or until tender, stirring occasionally. Add vinegar.

In large bowl combine the drained pasta with the mushroom mixture. Add as much reserved pasta water as needed to moisten. Toss with Parmesan cheese.

rves 5

cipe Note: Look for dark-brown portobellos with strong stalks. Avoid those h dark gills. Store in a loosely covered bowl in the refrigerator for up to days. Portobellos are a an ideal choice for vegetarian main courses. adapting your favorite eggplant recipes, and enjoy the flavorful results.

r Serving: 232 calories, 29g carbohydrate, 9g protein, 9g fat, 3g fiber, g cholesterol, 191mg sodium

© 2006 rights reserved by TRY-FOODS INTERNATIONAL Apopka, FL
The nutritional values and information provided are approximations.
Printed with soy-based inks. 08/07/06 #08257B_PPoP

STEAM-ROASTED CHICKEN

I was surprised to find out how fast and easy it is to roast a whole chicken with a pressure cooker. The chicken does not have a crisp skin, as is common with oven roasting, but the super-succulent results make it well worth the effort.

2 tbs. olive oil
1 tbs. butter
1 chicken, about 4 lb.
salt and pepper to taste

seasonings to taste, such as Old Bay,
   poultry seasoning or other favorite
   combination of herbs or spices
1 cup water

Heat oil and butter in a skillet over medium-high heat and brown chicken well on all sides. Place the trivet in the pressure cooker. Sprinkle chicken with salt, pepper and seasonings and place on trivet. Add water. Seal cooker, bring up to high pressure, reduce heat to stabilize pressure and cook for 5 minutes for each pound of chicken.

Remove cooker from heat and release pressure. Let chicken stand for 15 minutes before carving into serving pieces.

NOTE: Because of the minimum amount of liquid in this recipe, it may be necessary to increase the temperature slightly to maintain pressure.

LOW-FAT CHICKEN CACCIATORE

This is a very fast and easy recipe, which, because of the low-fat ingredients and skinless chicken, should fit into most diet plans.

2 lb. chicken pieces, skinned
1/4 tsp. salt
1/4 tsp. pepper
1/2 cup minced onion
2 cloves garlic, finely minced

1/2 cup dry red wine
1 can (28 oz.) whole plum tomatoes,
   coarsely chopped, with juice
1 tsp. dried basil
1 tsp. dried oregano

Sprinkle chicken with salt and pepper. Coat a nonstick skillet with vegetable spray and heat over medium-high heat. Add chicken and brown lightly on all sides. Remove chicken and coat skillet again with vegetable spray. Sauté onion over medium heat until softened; add a little water if onion is browning too quickly. Transfer chicken and onion to the pressure cooker. Stir in garlic, wine, tomatoes, basil and oregano and bring to a boil. Seal cooker, bring up to high pressure, reduce heat to stabilize pressure and cook for 10 minutes.

Remove cooker from heat and release pressure. Transfer chicken to a serving platter and keep warm. Simmer sauce uncovered until it thickens slightly, about 15 minutes. Taste sauce and adjust seasonings. Serve sauce over chicken.

CHICKEN ADOBO

This popular Filipino dish can be made in minutes with a pressure cooker. I like to serve brown rice as an accompaniment for the additional nutrition and fiber. Consider serving a colorful platter of steamed mixed vegetables as well.

1 chicken, about 3 lb., cut into serving
   pieces and skinned
1/2 cup cider vinegar
2 tsp. salt
1/2 cup water
1/4 tsp. pepper

1 bay leaf
3 cloves garlic, minced
1-2 tsp. grated fresh ginger
1 cup coconut milk
salt and pepper to taste, optional

Place the trivet in the pressure cooker and add all ingredients, except coconut milk. Seal cooker, bring up to high pressure, reduce heat to stabilize pressure and cook for 12 minutes.

Remove cooker from heat and release pressure. Transfer chicken to a serving dish; keep warm. Bring cooking liquid to a boil and cook uncovered until reduced to about half the original volume. Add coconut milk and simmer gently for 2 additional minutes. Taste and adjust seasonings; remove bay leaf. Pour thickened sauce over chicken.

STUFFED ROSEMARY CHICKEN

This chicken is stuffed with a subtle rosemary-flavored meat mixture that will make your guests' mouths water.

3 tbs. butter
1 small onion, minced
2 cloves garlic, minced
1 slice bread, soaked in milk
1/4 lb. ground beef
1/2 lb. ground veal
1/2 cup grated Parmesan cheese
1 egg
1 tsp. dried rosemary
1/2 tsp. dried thyme
2 tbs. minced fresh parsley
1 chicken, about 3 1/2 lb.
2 boneless chicken breast halves

melted butter
2 tsp. ground rosemary
salt and pepper to taste
vegetable oil
1 1/2 cups water

Heat butter in a skillet over medium heat and sauté onion and garlic until softened. Squeeze milk out of bread and mix bread with sautéed onion and garlic in a bowl. Add beef, veal, Parmesan, egg, rosemary, thyme and parsley; mix well.

With poultry shears or a large knife, cut through back of chicken. Open chicken and place meat filling down center of chicken. Place chicken breast pieces over filling so that back pieces close over breast pieces. Secure back pieces together with skewers, or sew together in a zigzag pattern with a trussing needle and kitchen string. Brush chicken with melted butter and sprinkle with 2 tsp. ground rosemary, salt and pepper. Heat enough oil to coat skillet over medium-high heat and brown chicken well on all sides.

Place stuffed chicken on the trivet in the pressure cooker and add water. Bring to a boil. Seal cooker, bring up to high pressure, reduce heat to stabilize pressure and cook for 8 minutes per pound of chicken (weight of chicken before stuffing).

Remove cooker from heat and release pressure. Transfer chicken to a cutting board. Let chicken stand for 15 minutes before carving into serving pieces.

BASQUE GAME HENS

This is a fast way to prepare a beautiful meal. Serve half or whole hens smothered in vegetables with a rice pilaf and a crisp green salad.

2 Cornish game hens, 1½ lb. each
2 tbs. flour
1 tsp. salt
¼ tsp. pepper
¼ tsp. chili powder
3 tbs. olive oil
1 medium onion, sliced
1 small eggplant, peeled and cubed
1 green bell pepper, cut into strips
1 cup sliced white mushrooms

2 cloves garlic, finely chopped
1 jar (4 oz.) sliced pimientos, drained
1 bay leaf
½ tsp. dried thyme
½ tsp. dried basil
½ tsp. salt
¼ tsp. pepper
2 cups dry white wine
1 tbs. capers
½ cup chopped Greek olives

Rinse and dry hens. In a small bowl, mix together flour, salt, pepper and chili powder and coat hens with mixture. In a large skillet, heat oil over medium-high heat and brown hens well on all sides. Remove hens from skillet and set aside. Add onion, eggplant, green pepper, mushrooms, garlic and pimientos to skillet and sauté over medium heat until vegetables are tender, about 3 minutes.

Place browned hens on the trivet or in the steamer basket in the pressure cooker. Cover with vegetables and sprinkle with bay leaf, thyme, basil, salt and pepper. Add wine and bring to a boil. Seal cooker, bring up to high pressure, reduce heat to stabilize pressure and cook for 12 to 15 minutes.

Remove cooker from heat and release pressure. Stir capers and olives into vegetables, remove bay leaf and transfer to a serving platter with game hens.

PAELLA

This is a fantastic, elegant meal that impresses everyone. I serve this in a large, flat, round dish, placing the rice in the bottom and artfully displaying the meats and fish on top. Serve with a nice tossed salad and crusty French bread.

1½ tsp. dried oregano
¼ tsp. pepper
1 clove garlic, minced
2 tsp. salt
3 tbs. olive oil
1½ tsp. wine vinegar
2 lb. chicken wings
¾ cup butter
1½ onions, diced
2¼ cups long-grain rice
3 cups chicken stock or water
6 chicken bouillon cubes
salt and pepper to taste
2 cloves garlic, minced

⅛ tsp. saffron threads
½ tsp. dried thyme
1 tbs. tomato paste
vegetable oil
1 cup frozen peas
1 cup marinated artichoke bottoms
2 tbs. capers
1 jar (2½ oz.) pimiento strips
½ lb. cooked shrimp
½ lb. cooked hot or mild Italian
   sausage, cut into chunks
assorted cooked seafood, such as clams,
   mussels and/or crab, optional

Mix oregano, pepper, 1 clove garlic, 2 tsp. salt, olive oil and vinegar together. With a knife, separate chicken wings at each joint and discard wing tips. Pour marinade over chicken pieces in a bowl and set aside.

Melt butter in the pressure cooker over medium heat and sauté onions until softened. Remove onions, add rice and sauté until rice turns golden brown. Return onions to cooker, add chicken stock, bouillon cubes, salt, pepper, 2 cloves garlic, saffron, thyme and tomato paste. Seal cooker, bring up to high pressure, reduce heat to stabilize pressure and cook for 10 minutes.

In a skillet, sauté marinated chicken wings over medium-high heat until golden brown and cooked through. Remove cooker from heat and release pressure. Add peas, artichoke bottoms, capers and ½ of the pimientos. Cook uncovered for about 1 minute until peas are heated through.

Heat broiler if desired. Spread rice mixture in a low, flat serving dish and arrange chicken pieces, shrimp, sausage pieces, remaining pimiento strips and seafood, if using, on top. If meats need a little warming, place dish under a broiler for a few minutes. Serve immediately.

SWEET AND SOUR FISH

Fish takes just minutes to cook with a pressure cooker. This sauce is light and delicate, so you can appreciate the true flavor of the fish. Serve with hot cooked rice.

2 green onions
1 cucumber
1 onion
3 slices fresh ginger
1 tsp. salt
6 tbs. sugar
½ cup white vinegar
½ cup water
2 tbs. vegetable oil
1 clove garlic, minced
1 tbs. hoisin sauce

2 tbs. rice vinegar
2 tbs. cornstarch
¼ cup water
2 lb. large fish fillets, such as cod or red snapper, or whole rainbow trout, cleaned and scaled
½ tsp. salt
dash white pepper
1 tbs. chopped fresh cilantro
2 tbs. sesame oil

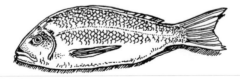

Slice green onions lengthwise into thin strips, 2 inches long. Peel and seed cucumber and cut into matchstick strips. Cut onion in half lengthwise and cut into matchstick strips. Peel ginger and cut into slivers. Mix 1 tsp. salt, sugar and white vinegar together. Pour over vegetable strips and let stand for 10 minutes. Add 1/2 cup water to marinade and let stand for 30 minutes; drain and reserve liquid.

Heat oil in a skillet and add garlic, hoisin sauce, rice vinegar and reserved marinade; bring to a boil. Dissolve cornstarch in 1/4 cup water and add to heated marinade mixture; stir until thickened.

Place fish on a piece of parchment paper or aluminum foil and place in the steamer basket in the pressure cooker. Sprinkle fish with 1/2 tsp. salt, white pepper and cilantro. Seal cooker, bring up to high pressure, reduce heat to stabilize pressure and cook for 3 minutes.

Remove cooker from heat and release pressure. Carefully transfer fish to a serving platter. Mix marinated vegetables with heated marinade and pour over fish. Sprinkle with sesame oil and serve immediately.

PRESSURE-STEAMED FISH IN BLACK BEAN SAUCE

Black beans compliment the subtleness of the fish beautifully. Fermented black beans are available in jars in Chinese markets or in the specialty food section of many supermarkets.

2 lb. firm white fish fillets, such as cod, red snapper or Chilean sea bass
1 tsp. salt
2 tsp. fermented black beans, rinsed
2 cloves garlic, minced
4 slices fresh ginger
1½ tbs. soy sauce
1 tbs. dry sherry
1 tsp. sugar
4 green onions, minced
½ cup water

Clean and skin fish, rinse and pat dry. Measure the thickness of fish at its thickest part and note measurement. Slash fish diagonally at ¾-inch intervals on both sides, cutting almost to the bone. Rub fish well with salt, both inside and out and including slashes, and lay on a shallow baking dish that fits inside the pressure cooker on the trivet.

Mince black beans with garlic and ginger and mix with soy sauce, sherry and sugar. Spoon black bean mixture over fish and sprinkle with ½ of the green onions. Pour water in cooker. Seal cooker, bring up to high pressure, reduce heat to stabilize pressure and cook for 5 minutes for every inch of thickness of fish.

Remove cooker from heat and release pressure. Test fish for doneness: flesh should be opaque. Remove cooked green onions and replace with remaining fresh green onions.

LINGUINI WITH SEAFOOD SAUCE

Make this great, quick red sauce any time of the year. Use fresh tomatoes whenever possible.

2 tbs. olive oil
2 onions, diced
2 tbs. finely chopped fresh parsley
2 cloves garlic, minced
2 cups chopped fresh tomatoes, or 1 can (32 oz.) tomato sauce
1½ lb. linguini
1 can (28 oz.) chopped clams, drained, or ¾ lb. cooked shrimp, halved
¼ cup chopped celery leaves, optional

Heat oil in the pressure cooker over medium heat and sauté onions and parsley until onions are softened. Add garlic and sauté for 1 minute. Add tomatoes and stir well. Seal cooker, bring up to high pressure, reduce heat to stabilize pressure and cook for 10 minutes.

Cook linguini according to package directions until slightly firm to the bite, *al dente*. Remove cooker from heat and release pressure. Stir in clams or shrimp. Pour sauce over linguini. For a mild celery flavor, add celery leaves to sauce just before serving.

CALICO BEANS

I adapted this recipe to the pressure cooker to make a quick, delicious and colorful mixed bean and meat dish. Serve with baked brown bread or cornbread.

1 lb. ground beef
½ lb. bacon, chopped
1 cup chopped onion
½ cup ketchup
1 tsp. salt
¾ cup brown sugar, packed, or more to taste
2 tsp. red wine vinegar or balsamic vinegar, or more to taste

1½ tsp. Dijon mustard
1 can (15½ oz.) pork and beans
1 can (10 oz.) garbanzo beans, rinsed and drained
1 can (15 oz.) kidney or pinto beans, rinsed and drained
1 can (15 oz.) lima or navy beans, rinsed and drained

Brown ground beef and chopped bacon in a skillet over medium-high heat. Add chopped onion and sauté until onions are softened. Transfer to the pressure cooker and mix in remaining ingredients. Stir well. Seal cooker, bring up to medium pressure, reduce heat to stabilize pressure and cook for 10 minutes.

Remove cooker from heat and release pressure. Taste and adjust sugar, vinegar and/or seasonings.

RABBIT IN MUSHROOM-WINE SAUCE

Don't be afraid of trying rabbit. It tastes very much like chicken, with even less fat. You can, however, substitute chicken for the rabbit if you wish.

1 rabbit, 2½-3 lb.
salt and pepper
3 tbs. olive oil
2 tbs. butter
1 medium onion, chopped
2-3 cloves garlic, minced
½ cup dry white wine
½ cup Marsala wine
¼ cup chicken stock

1 tsp. ground rosemary
¼ tsp. dried thyme
1 tbs. butter
1 tbs. olive oil
¾ lb. sliced white mushrooms
2 tbs. minced fresh parsley
salt and pepper to taste
1 tbs. cornstarch, optional
1 tbs. water, optional

Cut rabbit into serving pieces and sprinkle with salt and pepper. Heat 3 tbs. olive oil and 2 tbs. butter in a skillet over medium-high heat and brown rabbit pieces on all sides. Transfer browned pieces to the pressure cooker. Add onion, garlic, white wine, Marsala wine, chicken stock, rosemary and thyme. Bring mixture to a low boil and cook uncovered for 5 minutes. Seal cooker, bring up to high pressure, reduce heat to stabilize pressure and cook for 30 minutes.

In another skillet, heat 1 tbs. butter and 1 tbs. oil over medium-high heat. Sauté mushrooms, parsley, salt and pepper until mushrooms soften. Remove cooker from heat and release pressure. Add cooked mushroom mixture to cooker. Remove rabbit pieces and place on a serving platter; keep warm.

To thicken sauce, simmer uncovered until reduced and thickened. Or, dissolve cornstarch in water and add to simmering sauce. Cook, stirring, for about 1 minute to thicken. Pour sauce over rabbit and serve immediately.

VEGETABLES

ABOUT PRESSURE COOKING VEGETABLES

- Use the steamer basket whenever possible to keep vegetables out of the cooking water. This way, the vitamins do not leach into the water.

- To avoid overcooking, use the minimum amount of water required by the manufacturer and bring it to a boil before sealing the cooker. Distribute the vegetables evenly in the steamer basket to ensure even cooking.

- Vegetables cook very quickly in a pressure cooker, so watch the time closely. When adapting recipes, keep the cooking time to a minimum, usually about 1/3 the time of cooking conventionally.

- If using frozen vegetables, generally use the same amount of water called for in the recipe, but increase the cooking time by about 1/2 over fresh vegetables.

- When cooking more than one vegetable, cut the shorter-cooking vegetables in larger pieces than the longer-cooking vegetables. Or, partially cook the longer-cooking vegetables first, release the pressure and add the remaining vegetables; reseal the cooker, repressurize and continue cooking.

- For best results, use the *Quick Release Method*, page 5, for releasing pressure-cooked vegetables and serve the vegetables immediately.

VEGETABLE COOKING TIMES*

VEGETABLE TYPE	MINUTES (after reaching full pressure)
Artichokes, large	9 to 11
Asparagus	0**
Beets, small-medium, whole	12 to 15
Broccoli, large florets	2
Brussels sprouts	2 to 3
Cabbage wedges	5 to 7
Carrot slices	2
Cauliflower, large florets	1 to 2
Corn ears, fresh	2 to 3
Eggplant slices	1 to 2
Onions, medium, whole	5 to 10
Parsnips, chunks	2 to 5
Potatoes, red, small-medium	4 to 7
Squash, winter, halved	10 to 15
Squash, spaghetti	15 to 18
Squash, summer	0**
Sweet potatoes, quartered	8 to 12
Turnips, chunks	4 to 5

*Based on high pressure
**Bring up to high pressure, remove from heat, release pressure and serve immediately.

EGGPLANT AND OLIVE SPREAD

Servings: 8-12

The Italian name for this is caponata, which is great served with sliced French bread or crackers. I like to serve it as a yummy vegetable side dish. Serve hot or cold.

1 large eggplant, peeled and cut into cubes
salt
1/4 cup olive oil
1 zucchini, diced
1 large onion, diced
3 cloves garlic, minced
1/2 cup chopped celery
1 carrot, chopped
1 green bell pepper, chopped
1 1/2 cups chopped fresh tomatoes

1/4 cup chopped fresh parsley
2-3 tbs. tomato paste
1 1/2 tsp. dried basil
1/4 cup balsamic vinegar
1 tsp. sugar
1/4 cup pimiento-stuffed green olives
1/2 cup pitted Greek olives
2 tbs. capers
salt and pepper to taste

Sprinkle eggplant with salt, place in a colander and drain for 30 minutes. Heat oil in the pressure cooker over medium-high heat and sauté eggplant and zucchini until lightly browned. Stir in onion, garlic, celery and carrot and sauté for 5 minutes. Add remaining ingredients and bring to a boil, stirring constantly. Seal cooker, bring up to medium pressure, reduce heat to stabilize pressure and cook for 20 minutes.

Remove from heat and release pressure. Taste and adjust seasonings.

TRI-COLOR PEPPER SPREAD

This is a wonderful Italian appetizer, which has been adapted to the pressure cooker. Serve it with crusty French bread.

1 red bell pepper
1 green bell pepper
1 yellow bell pepper
1/2 cup water
olive oil

pepper to taste
2 tbs. capers
1 tbs. anchovy paste
1/2 cup chopped Greek olives
sliced French bread

Cut peppers into matchstick strips. Place in the steamer basket in the pressure cooker and add water. Seal cooker, bring up to high pressure, reduce heat to stabilize pressure and cook for 3 minutes.

Remove cooker from heat and release pressure. Remove steamer basket and pour out excess water; wipe cooker dry. Coat bottom of cooker with olive oil and add steamed pepper mixture. Sauté over medium-high heat until peppers are browned. Add pepper, capers, anchovy paste and olives. Taste and adjust seasonings. Serve warm with slices of French bread.

WINTER VEGETABLE DIP

This sweet, spicy vegetarian dip is good served with assorted vegetables, crackers or pita bread. You can also serve this warm as a starchy vegetable side dish.

1 lb. carrots
1 lb. sweet potatoes
1 cup water
3 cloves garlic, minced
1 tsp. ground cumin
1 tsp. cinnamon
¼ cup olive oil
3 tbs. wine vinegar
pinch cayenne pepper, or dash Tabasco Sauce

Peel carrots and sweet potatoes and cut into small pieces. Place vegetables in the steamer basket in the pressure cooker along with water. Bring to a boil. Seal cooker, bring up to high pressure, reduce heat to stabilize pressure and cook for 10 minutes.

Remove cooker from heat and release pressure. Puree cooked vegetables with a blender or food processor and mix with remaining ingredients. Taste and adjust seasonings.

BRAISED ORANGE FENNEL

Fennel is reminiscent of licorice and goes especially well with orange juice. Serve with colorful steamed vegetables and a sauced meat dish.

4 bulbs fennel
½ cup water
2 tbs. butter
2 tsp. brown sugar

1 clove garlic, minced
½ cup orange juice
salt and pepper to taste

Cut fennel bulbs in half. Place bulbs in the steamer basket in the pressure cooker with water. Seal cooker, bring up to high pressure, reduce heat to stabilize pressure and cook for 3 to 5 minutes, depending on the size of bulbs.

Remove cooker from heat and release pressure. Remove fennel, pour out any remaining water from cooker and wipe dry. Melt butter in cooker over medium-high heat and add sugar, stirring to dissolve. Add garlic and partially cooked fennel bulbs. Cook until nicely browned on one side. Turn bulbs over and add orange juice, salt and pepper. When second side is nicely browned, remove from heat and serve immediately.

PROSCIUTTO-WRAPPED LEEKS

Servings: 4-6

This quick, elegant vegetable dish can be made ahead of time, placed in a casserole dish, sprinkled with Parmesan and broiled to reheat at the last minute. It's ideal for cooks on the run!

2 lb. large leeks
1/2 cup water
1/4 lb. prosciutto, sliced very thinly

1/4 cup butter, melted
1/2 cup grated Parmesan cheese
salt and pepper to taste

Cut off tough green upper portion of leeks and pare root end. Cut stalks in half lengthwise and thoroughly wash out sand and grit under cold running water; root end should stay intact. Carefully lay leek halves in the steamer basket in the pressure cooker and add water. Seal cooker, bring up to high pressure, reduce heat to stabilize pressure and cook for about 2 minutes.

Remove from heat and release pressure. To serve at once, heat broiler. Wrap each leek section with a slice of prosciutto, place in a baking dish, drizzle with melted butter and sprinkle with Parmesan, salt and pepper. Place dish under broiler until cheese is browned slightly.

To serve later, rinse steamed leeks in cold water and pat dry before wrapping with prosciutto. Add remaining ingredients, refrigerate and broil just before serving.

EGGPLANT PARMESAN

Servings: 6-8

This is a vegetarian dish that even meat eaters enjoy. Both the sauce and the finished dish can be prepared in the pressure cooker. However, you can also bake the casserole in its final stage: Heat the oven to 375° and bake covered casserole for 45 minutes to 1 hour.

2 large eggplants
salt
2 tbs. olive oil
1 onion, chopped
2 cloves garlic, minced
¼ cup dry red wine
1 can (8 oz.) tomato sauce
1½ cups chopped fresh tomatoes, or
   1 can (16 oz.) whole plum tomatoes
1 tsp. dried basil
1 tsp. dried oregano
olive oil for brushing
salt and pepper to taste
¾ cup grated Parmesan cheese
6 oz. Monterey Jack or mozzarella cheese, shredded

Slice eggplants into ¼-inch rounds. Sprinkle rounds with salt and drain in a colander while preparing sauce.

Heat oil in the pressure cooker over medium heat. Sauté onion and garlic until softened. Add wine and simmer for 5 minutes. Add tomato sauce, chopped tomatoes, basil and oregano and bring to a boil. Seal cooker, bring up to high pressure, reduce heat to stabilize pressure and cook for 15 minutes.

Remove cooker from heat and release pressure. Taste sauce and adjust seasonings. Transfer sauce to a bowl and clean pressure cooker.

Heat broiler. Wipe eggplant slices dry, brush lightly with a little olive oil, sprinkle with salt and pepper and broil until lightly browned. Oil a casserole dish that fits in pressure cooker. Layer ingredients in the following order until all are used, ending with a layer of cheese: sauce, eggplant, sauce, cheese. Cover entire dish with aluminum foil, sealing the edges well. Place covered casserole dish on trivet in pressure cooker and add water. Seal cooker, bring up to high pressure, reduce heat to stabilize pressure and cook for 15 to 20 minutes.

Heat broiler if desired. Remove cooker from heat and release pressure. If desired, place casserole under broiler for a few minutes to brown cheese.

RATATOUILLE WITH RICE

Ratatouille is a popular dish from the Provence region of France, which combines eggplant and a variety of vegetables. Use this variation, which adds rice and cheese for substance, as a side dish or a main entrée for a vegetarian meal.

4 cups water
1 tsp. salt
1 cup long-grain rice
1/2 cup olive oil
1 lb. onions, sliced
1 lb. eggplant, peeled and cubed
1 1/2 lb. zucchini, diced
1 cup sliced green bell pepper
4 lb. tomatoes, peeled and sliced
salt and pepper to taste
1/2 cup chicken stock
5 cloves garlic, crushed
2 tbs. chopped fresh parsley
2 tbs. chopped fresh basil
1/2 cup grated Gruyère or Parmesan cheese

Bring water and salt to a boil in the pressure cooker. Add rice and cook uncovered for 7 minutes. Drain and refresh rice under cold running water; drain thoroughly.

Wipe cooker dry, add olive oil and sauté sliced onions over medium heat until softened. Add eggplant, zucchini, green pepper, 1/2 of the tomato slices, parboiled rice and remaining tomato slices. Season with salt and pepper on each layer. Add chicken stock, garlic, parsley and basil. Heat mixture gently, stirring until bubbling. Seal cooker, bring up to high pressure, reduce heat to stabilize pressure and cook for 3 to 4 minutes.

Heat broiler. Remove cooker from heat and release pressure. Transfer vegetables to an ovenproof dish and sprinkle with cheese. Place under broiler for a few minutes to melt cheese.

SPINACH ARTICHOKE CASSEROLE

This is a favorite vegetable dish to bring to potluck parties. Your friends will never believe that spinach could be so delicious!

1 pkg. (¾ oz.) Italian salad dressing mix
½ cup olive oil
½ cup cider vinegar of balsamic vinegar
2 large cans (15 oz.) artichoke hearts, drained and cut into quarters
6 pkg. (10 oz. each) frozen chopped spinach, thawed and squeezed very dry
16 oz. cream cheese, softened
2 tbs. mayonnaise
1-1½ cups grated Parmesan cheese
½ cup water

Mix salad dressing mix with olive oil and vinegar. Pour mixture over artichokes in a bowl. If time permits, marinate artichokes for several hours.

Butter a 6- or 8-cup deep casserole dish that fits in the pressure cooker. Spread 1/3 of the spinach in dish. Arrange 1/3 of the marinated artichokes over spinach and drizzle with a little marinade. Mix softened cream cheese with mayonnaise and spread 1/3 of the mixture over artichokes. Repeat this procedure 2 more times. Sprinkle top of casserole with Parmesan cheese. Cover top of dish with waxed paper and cover entire dish with aluminum foil, sealing the edges well. Place covered casserole on trivet in pressure cooker and add water. Seal cooker, bring up to high pressure, reduce heat to stabilize pressure and cook for 20 minutes.

Heat broiler. Remove cooker from heat and release pressure. Remove foil and waxed paper from dish. Place dish under broiler for a few minutes to brown cheese.

SWEET POTATO PUREE

You can substitute orange peel for lemon peel and orange juice for cream for an interesting variation on this dish.

3 medium sweet potatoes or yams
1 cup water
2 tbs. butter, melted
2-3 tbs. heavy cream
finely grated peel (zest) of 1 large lemon
salt to taste

Scrub sweet potatoes well. Pierce skin with a fork several times and place in the steamer basket or on the trivet in the pressure cooker. Add water and bring to a boil. Seal cooker, bring up to high pressure, reduce heat to stabilize pressure and cook for about 12 minutes.

Remove cooker from heat and release pressure. Peel sweet potatoes and cut into small pieces. Press through a ricer or food grinder, or beat with a mixer just until smooth. Add remaining ingredients and mix well. Taste and adjust seasonings.

WINTER SQUASH PUREE

Use butternut, acorn, hubbard or banana squash, but allow a greater amount of cooking time for thicker-fleshed types. For variety, use a little cinnamon or ground cloves in place of the other spices. For a thinner puree, add a few tablespoons of cream or orange juice.

1 medium winter squash
1 cup water
2 tbs. butter, melted
1-2 tbs. brown sugar
pinch nutmeg

pinch ground ginger
salt to taste
chopped toasted pecans for garnish,
    optional

Cut squash in half and remove seeds and any stringy fibers. Place squash in the steamer basket or on the trivet in the pressure cooker, add water and bring to a boil. Seal cooker, bring up to high pressure, reduce heat to stabilize pressure and cook for 10 to 12 minutes.

Remove cooker from heat and release pressure. Remove skin from squash. Cut squash flesh into small pieces. Press squash through a ricer or food grinder, or beat with a mixer just until smooth. Stir in remaining ingredients, taste and adjust seasonings.

PARSNIP, CARROT AND POTATO PUREE

Makes: 4 cups

Once you turn vegetables into a puree, they appear more like a creamy dessert than a vegetable, which is appreciated by children. This recipe is a mixture of purees, but each vegetable can be pureed separately using the same technique.

1 lb. parsnips
½ lb. carrots
¾ lb. potatoes
½ cup water
salt and pepper to taste
¼ cup butter
½ cup heavy cream

Peel vegetables and cut into cubes. Place vegetables in the steamer basket in the pressure cooker with water. Seal cooker, bring up to high pressure, reduce heat to stabilize pressure and cook for 10 minutes.

Remove cooker from heat and release pressure. Place cooked vegetables in a food processor workbowl or blender container. Add salt, pepper, butter and cream and puree just until smooth; do not overmix or mixture will become sticky. Taste and adjust seasonings.

GINGERED CARROTS

Parsnips can be substituted or mixed in with this recipe. Changing the flavor of the fruit vinegar adds a subtle change. Ginger adds heat to a dish, so if you like a little more kick, increase the amount of ginger used.

6 medium carrots
1 cup water
1 tbs. butter
2 large slices fresh ginger, about 1/8-inch thick, cut into fine slivers
1/4 cup chicken stock
1 1/2 tbs. raspberry vinegar
salt and pepper to taste

Peel carrots and slice into long matchstick strips. Place in the steamer basket or on the trivet in the pressure cooker along with water and bring to a boil. Seal cooker, bring up to high pressure, reduce heat to stabilize pressure and cook for 2 to 3 minutes.

Remove cooker from heat and release pressure. Rinse carrots under cold running water to stop the cooking process; drain well.

Heat butter in a skillet over medium-high heat and add carrots and ginger. Cook for 1 minute, add stock and boil until most of the stock is evaporated. Stir in vinegar, taste and adjust seasonings.

CARROT AND ONION MEDLEY

Onions are a great compliment to carrots. With pressure cooking, this dish can be made in minutes. Try this with roasted chicken and mashed potatoes.

1/4 cup butter
3 medium onions, sliced
1 tbs. flour
1 1/2 lb. carrots, cut into matchstick strips
3/4 cup chicken stock
1 tsp. sugar
salt and pepper to taste

Melt butter in the pressure cooker over medium heat. Add onions and sauté until softened. Add flour and sauté for 1 minute. Add remaining ingredients. Seal cooker, bring up to high pressure, reduce heat to stabilize pressure and cook for 2 to 3 minutes.

Remove cooker from heat and release pressure. Test carrots for doneness. If additional cooking is required, cook carrots uncovered until tender. Taste and adjust seasonings.

BROCCOLI-STUFFED ONIONS

Consider something totally different the next time you have special guests for dinner. These onions are pressure cooked until tender and filled with a creamy broccoli mixture.

4 large Spanish onions
pinch salt
1 cup water
1 pkg. (10 oz.) frozen chopped broccoli

$2/3$ cup grated Parmesan cheese
$1/2$ cup mayonnaise
1 tsp. lemon juice
salt and pepper to taste

Cut onions in half crosswise. Place halves in the steamer basket in the pressure cooker, sprinkle with salt and pour in water. Seal cooker, bring up to high pressure, reduce heat to stabilize pressure and cook for 6 to 8 minutes.

Remove cooker from heat and release pressure. Remove steamer basket and let onions drain and cool.

Heat oven to 375°. Cook broccoli according to package directions until tender-crisp; drain. Remove centers of onions, leaving a $3/4$-inch wall. Chop centers of onions and mix with broccoli, Parmesan, mayonnaise, lemon juice, salt and pepper. Mound broccoli mixture inside onion shells. Place filled onions in a greased baking dish and bake uncovered for 20 minutes.

PECAN ONION FLOWERS

For a unique vegetable dish, serve onions cut like chrysanthemums, which are steamed and drizzled with butter and pecans.

6 large onions
1 cup water
6 tbs. butter, melted
2 tbs. sugar or brown sugar
salt and pepper to taste
3 tbs. chopped pecans

Make multiple slits in onions, from top to root end, cutting only ¾ through. Place onions root-end down in the steamer basket in the pressure cooker, add water and bring to a boil. Seal cooker, bring up to high pressure, reduce heat to stabilize pressure and cook for 8 to 10 minutes.

Heat oven to 350°. Remove cooker from heat and release pressure. Remove steamer basket and let onions drain and cool. Very carefully remove onions with a slotted spoon and place in a baking dish. Drizzle onions with melted butter and sprinkle with sugar, salt, pepper and pecans. Bake for 30 minutes.

SWEET AND SOUR CABBAGE

For a change, use both red and green cabbage for this recipe. Both versions go great with garlic mashed potatoes.

2 tbs. butter
2 cloves garlic, minced
1 onion, sliced
4 cups sliced red cabbage
½ tsp. salt
pepper to taste
1½ tsp. caraway seeds
1 bay leaf
½ cup dry red wine
1 tbs. sugar
½ cup water

Melt butter in the pressure cooker over medium heat. Add garlic and onion and sauté until softened. Add remaining ingredients and bring to a boil. Seal cooker, bring up to high pressure, reduce heat to stabilize pressure and cook for 3 to 4 minutes.

Remove cooker from heat and release pressure. Remove bay leaf, taste and adjust seasonings.

ORANGE-GLAZED BEETS

Beets can be quite plain, but add a little orange and even kids can appreciate them. If you wish, serve with a small dollop of sour cream.

12 medium beets, tops removed
1 cup water
2 tbs. butter
5 tbs. sugar
1 tbs. cornstarch
1 tsp. salt, or more to taste
1 cup orange juice
orange slices or strips of orange peel (zest) for garnish, optional

Place beets in the steamer basket in the pressure cooker with water and bring to a boil. Seal cooker, bring up to high pressure, reduce heat to stabilize pressure and cook for 15 minutes.

In a saucepan, melt butter over medium-high heat. Stir in sugar, cornstarch and salt. Add orange juice and stir until thickened.

Remove cooker from heat and release pressure. Peel beets and cut into slices or chunks. Place in a serving dish and cover with orange sauce. Garnish with orange slices or thin strips of orange peel.

SIDE DISHES

ABOUT PRESSURE COOKING RICE AND BEANS

- See page 33 for tips on pressure cooking rice.

- *For plain rice*, bring water to a boil and add rice. Cook under high pressure for 6 to 7 minutes for white rice and about 18 minutes for brown rice. Brown rice can be soaked in water to cover for at least 1 hour. This reduces the cooking time to about 12 minutes; reduce the liquid in the recipe by $1/2$ cup.

- *For rice pilaf*, heat oil in cooker and sauté rice until it is golden brown. Add vegetables and sauté until softened. Add liquid and bring to a boil; proceed as for standard rice.

- Dried beans will double in volume when soaked. Take care to soak them in a container that is large enough to accommodate the quantity. Always keep beans in the refrigerator when soaking overnight.

- Although it is not necessary to presoak beans for pressure cooking, soaking does offer some advantages. Since the gas-producing qualities of beans are water-soluble, soaking reduces their effects. Always drain the soaking water from the beans and cook with fresh water. Soaking also cuts down the cooking time and keeps the bean skins from separating from the flesh.

- If you don't have time to soak beans overnight, use the *Hot Soaking Method*: Use 5 cups water and 2 tsp. salt for every 8 oz. dried beans. Place the ingredients in the pressure cooker and bring up to low pressure. Remove cooker from heat, release pressure and let stand for 4 hours. Drain and discard soaking water. At this point you may want to add a product called *Beano,* which reduces the gas-producing qualities of beans. It is available in most health food stores.

- When adapting bean recipes, use 3 cups fresh water for every 8 oz. beans for cooking; do not add salt at this stage or the beans will remain tough. Adding 1 tbs. oil will prevent the beans from clogging the pressure cooker's vents. Bring the cooker up to high pressure and cook according to the chart on page 126. If you wish to puree the beans, increase the cooking time by at least 50 percent.

- Do not exceed the fill mark of the pressure cooker when cooking any food.

- Always use the *Cold Water Release Method* (see page 5) when pressure cooking beans to prevent sputtering.

- Clean the lid and vents of the pressure cooker thoroughly after pressure cooking rice and beans.

COOKING TIMES FOR DRIED BEANS*

BEAN TYPE	PRESOAKED	UNSOAKED
	(minutes after reaching full pressure)	
Adzuki	6 to 8	15 to 20
Black	8 to 10	20 to 25
Black-eyed peas**	—	9 to 11
Calypso	4 to 6	22 to 25
Cranberry	9 to 12	30 to 35
Fava	12 to 18	22 to 28
Garbanzo	10 to 12	32 to 38
Great Northern	8 to 11	25 to 30
Kidney	9 to 12	20 to 25
Lentils (brown or green)**	—	8 to 12
Lentils (red)**	—	3 to 4
Lima	4 to 7	12 to 15
Navy	5 to 8	18 to 25
Peas, split	10 to 12	28 to 30
Pinto	5 to 7	22 to 25
Red	4 to 6	22 to 25
Soybeans	10 to 12	28 to 35

*Based on high pressure
**Not necessary to presoak

RICE WITH CARROTS AND APPLE

Here's a quick, colorful rice dish that goes well with pork and chicken entrées. The addition of fresh apple pieces adds an unusual refreshing flavor, as well as vibrant color. Use dried currants or golden raisins in place of dark raisins for a delicious variation.

1¾ cups water
¾ cup apple juice
¼ tsp. cinnamon
pinch salt
1½ cups long-grain rice
⅓ cup raisins

¼ cup butter
1 cup sliced carrots
1 large red apple, chopped
4 green onions, sliced
2 tbs. sesame seeds, toasted

Bring water, apple juice, cinnamon and salt to a boil in the pressure cooker. Add rice and raisins. Seal cooker, bring up to high pressure, reduce heat to stabilize pressure and cook for 6 minutes.

Heat butter in a skillet over medium heat and sauté carrots until tender. Remove cooker from heat and release pressure. Gently stir in cooked carrots, chopped fresh apple pieces, green onions and sesame seeds. Serve immediately.

SAVORY RICE AND ARTICHOKES

Use the basic rice preparation with different assorted vegetables for unlimited color, texture and variation. Add capers and chopped Greek olives for a piquant flavor.

1/4 cup olive oil
2 cups long-grain rice
1 onion, minced
2-3 cloves garlic, minced
3 1/4 cups chicken stock
salt and pepper to taste

1/8 tsp. saffron threads dissolved in
   1 tbs. water, optional
1 cup frozen peas, thawed
12 artichoke hearts, halved
1 jar (2 oz.) pimiento strips

Heat oil in the pressure cooker over medium heat. Add rice and sauté until golden brown. Add onion and garlic and sauté until softened. Add chicken stock, salt, pepper and saffron and bring to a boil. Seal cooker, bring up to high pressure, reduce heat to stabilize pressure and cook for 6 minutes.

Remove cooker from heat and release pressure. Taste and adjust seasonings. Add peas, artichoke hearts and pimiento strips. Stir gently with a fork until well mixed.

GREEK RICE PILAF

Spearmint, one of the unusual ingredients frequently used in Greek cooking, makes this pilaf different. It is great served with a salad of marinated vegetables, feta cheese and Greek olives.

1/4 cup butter
2 cups long-grain rice
1 qt. chicken stock
1 tsp. salt
1 tbs. dried parsley
1/2 tsp. dried spearmint
1/2 tsp. dried basil

Heat butter in the pressure cooker over medium heat. Add rice and sauté until golden brown. Add remaining ingredients and bring to a boil. Seal cooker, bring up to high pressure, reduce heat to stabilize pressure and cook for 6 minutes.

Remove cooker from heat and release pressure. Taste and adjust seasonings.

SWEET PEPPER RISOTTO

Risotto is made with Arborio rice, a short-grained Italian variety that takes on a naturally creamy texture when cooked. Cooking it conventionally takes about 30 minutes of constant attention. Pressure cooking reduces the long cooking time considerably and prevents the need to slowly add the liquid and stir continually throughout the cooking process.

2 tbs. olive oil
2 tbs. butter
1 cup diced onion
1½ cups Arborio rice
1 cup diced red, yellow and/or green bell peppers
½ cup dry white wine
4½ cups chicken stock
½ cup grated Parmesan or Asiago cheese
½ cup grated Romano cheese
½-1 cup pine nuts, toasted
½ cup sliced Greek or black olives, optional
1 tbs. chopped fresh parsley

Heat oil and butter in the pressure cooker over medium heat. Add onion and sauté until softened. Stir in rice until all grains are coated. Add peppers, wine and chicken stock, stir to combine and bring to a boil. Seal cooker, bring up to high pressure, reduce heat to stabilize pressure and cook for 6 minutes.

Remove cooker from heat and release pressure. Transfer risotto to a serving dish and stir in cheeses, pine nuts and olives, if using. Sprinkle with parsley and serve at once.

GREEN RICE

This is a good side dish for fish dishes or Mexican meals. It is quick, simple and a lot tastier than plain white rice. This is excellent served with a cheesy main dish and tender-crisp vegetables.

3 tbs. vegetable oil
1½ cups long-grain rice
8 canned mild green chiles
3 tbs. chopped fresh parsley
2 cloves garlic
3 cups chicken stock
salt and pepper to taste

Heat oil in the pressure cooker over medium heat and add rice. Sauté until rice is slightly browned; be careful not to scorch. With a food processor or blender, process chiles with parsley and garlic until smooth. Add mixture to rice with chicken stock and bring to a boil. Seal cooker, bring up to high pressure, reduce heat to stabilize pressure and cook for 5 minutes.

Remove cooker from heat and release pressure. Fluff rice gently with a fork. Add salt and pepper to taste.

MUSHROOM BARLEY PILAF

Consider a change from the typical potato or rice side dishes — have barley instead. For a more exotic dish, use wild mushrooms, such as chanterelles, morels and/or shiitakes. For a vegetarian dish, use vegetable stock instead of chicken stock.

½ cup butter
1¾ cups pearl barley
2 cups chopped onions
¾ lb. white or wild mushrooms, sliced

1 cup dry white wine
4 cups chicken stock
salt and pepper to taste
½ cup slivered almonds, toasted

Heat ½ of the butter in the pressure cooker over medium heat. Add barley and sauté until golden brown. Remove barley and set aside. Melt remaining butter in cooker and sauté onions and mushrooms over medium-high heat until softened. Return barley to cooker with wine, chicken stock, salt and pepper and bring to a boil. Seal cooker, bring up to high pressure, reduce heat to stabilize pressure and cook for 25 minutes.

Remove cooker from heat and release pressure using the *Cold Water Release Method* (see page 5). Gently stir in almonds with a fork. Serve immediately.

PASTA VEGETABLE MEDLEY

Pasta is a popular dish anywhere. This can be used either as a side dish or as a vegetarian main course. Serve with garlic bread, a crisp salad and a fruit dessert.

3 carrots
3 small zucchini
3 small yellow crookneck squash
1 tbs. olive oil
1 tbs. butter
2 cloves garlic, minced
1½ cups chopped fresh basil, or ½ cup dried
¾ cup minced fresh parsley
2 tbs. chopped fresh chives or finely chopped green onions
1 tsp. dried marjoram
1½ tsp. salt
½ cup water
1½ lb. white or whole wheat spaghetti
½ cup grated Parmesan cheese

Cut carrots, zucchini and yellow squash into long, thin strips to resemble the shape of spaghetti. Heat olive oil and butter in the pressure cooker over medium-high heat and add vegetables. Sauté for 1 minute. Add remaining ingredients, except spaghetti and Parmesan cheese. Seal cooker, bring up to high pressure, reduce heat to stabilize pressure and cook for 2 to 3 minutes.

Cook spaghetti according to instructions on package until slightly firm to the bite, *al dente*. Drain and transfer to a warm serving bowl.

Remove cooker from heat and release pressure. Immediately transfer vegetables to bowl with spaghetti; mix well and sprinkle with cheese. Toss, taste and adjust seasonings.

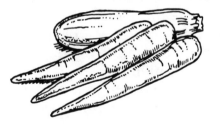

POTATOES AND LOX

This is an incredibly delicious potato dish that has an extra-special touch of smoked salmon for added flavor and color. Serve with a meat entrée and a green vegetable.

6 medium russet potatoes, peeled
salt and pepper to taste
1/4 cup minced Bermuda onion

1/4-1/2 lb. thinly sliced lox
2 cups heavy cream
1 cup water

Butter a casserole dish that fits in the pressure cooker. Thinly slice potatoes and lay 1/3 of the potatoes in dish. Sprinkle with salt, pepper and 1/2 of the minced onion. Layer 1/2 of the lox over potatoes. Repeat this procedure and finish by layering with remaining 1/3 potatoes. Pour cream evenly over potatoes. Cover entire dish with aluminum foil, sealing the edges well. Place dish in cooker on the trivet or in the steamer basket. Add water. Seal cooker, bring up to high pressure, reduce heat to stabilize pressure and cook for 20 minutes.

Heat broiler. Remove cooker from heat and release pressure. Remove foil from dish and place under broiler until top is lightly browned. Serve immediately.

NOTE: Avoid using too much onion, because it will curdle the cream.

SOUTHERN SWEET BEANS

These are incredibly quick and simple to make because you use canned beans. Traditionally, this dish is served over cornbread wedges. It is also good served over couscous or sweet potatoes. A crisp cucumber salad is a good accompaniment.

2 tbs. vegetable oil
1 green bell pepper, diced
1 red bell pepper, diced
1 onion, chopped
2-3 cloves garlic, minced
2 cans (15 oz. each) black, kidney,
    garbanzo, pinto or a mixture of beans

1 tbs. ground cumin
1/4 tsp. cayenne pepper, or more to
    taste
1/2 cup tomato sauce
1/4 cup raisins

Heat oil in the pressure cooker over medium-high heat. Add peppers, onion and garlic and sauté for 2 minutes. Add beans (undrained) and remaining ingredients and scrape bottom of cooker well. Bring to a boil. Seal cooker, bring up to medium pressure, reduce heat to stabilize pressure and cook for 5 minutes.

Remove cooker from heat and release pressure. Taste and adjust seasonings.

SWEET FIERY LENTILS

This can be used as side dish, or even a main dish, because lentils are a great protein source. If you wish to make this totally vegetarian, use vegetable stock instead of chicken stock in the recipe.

2 tbs. olive oil
1 red onion, sliced
1 yellow onion, sliced
2-3 cloves garlic, minced
1 tbs. cinnamon
1 tbs. ground ginger
1/4 tsp. cayenne pepper, or to taste

1/4 tsp. red pepper flakes, or to taste
2 bay leaves
2 cups green lentils
3 1/2 cups chicken stock
2 tbs. lemon juice
1 tbs. grated fresh lemon peel (zest)

Heat oil in the pressure cooker over medium heat and sauté onions and garlic until softened. Add remaining ingredients, except lemon juice and zest. Bring mixture to a boil. Seal cooker, bring up to high pressure, reduce heat to stabilize pressure and cook for 10 minutes.

Remove cooker from heat and release pressure using the *Cold Water Release Method* (see page 5). Stir in lemon juice and lemon peel and remove bay leaves. Taste and adjust seasonings.

LENTILS WITH ALMONDS AND CURRANTS

Instead of rice pilaf, consider making a lentil side dish. This could also be used as an entrée, served over potatoes with cranberry sauce as an accompaniment.

2 tbs. olive oil
1 cup red or yellow lentils
1 tsp. ground cardamom
1½ tsp. cinnamon
1 bay leaf
½ tsp. ground cumin
⅛ tsp. cayenne pepper

black pepper to taste
3 cups chicken stock
3 tbs. chopped toasted almonds
½ cup dried currants
½ cup sour cream or plain yogurt,
   or more to taste
salt to taste, optional

Heat olive oil in the pressure cooker over medium-high heat. Add lentils and sauté for 2 minutes. Add cardamom, cinnamon, bay leaf, cumin, cayenne, black pepper and chicken stock and bring to a boil. Seal cooker, bring up to high pressure, reduce heat to stabilize pressure and cook for 10 minutes.

Remove cooker from heat and release pressure using the *Cold Water Release Method* (see page 5). Stir in almonds, currants and sour cream, and remove bay leaf. Taste and adjust seasonings.

BOSTON-STYLE BROWN BREAD

Makes: 1 loaf

Sometimes my mother would serve this warm with butter or with traditional baked beans as an after-school treat. Brown bread also goes well with chicken and fruit salads. Be inventive with different flour mixtures for a delightful change. This bread is delicious spread with orange-flavored cream cheese.

1 cup all-purpose flour
1½ cups whole wheat or graham flour, or a combination of whole-wheat, graham
    and/or rye flour
½ cup cornmeal
½ tsp. salt
1 tsp. baking powder
1 tsp. baking soda
1 cup buttermilk
2 eggs, beaten
3 tbs. butter, melted
⅔ cup molasses
1¼ cups raisins
2 cups water

Combine flours, cornmeal, salt and baking powder. Mix baking soda with buttermilk and add beaten eggs. Mix melted butter with molasses and stir into buttermilk mixture. Add dry ingredients to buttermilk mixture and stir until well combined. Stir in raisins. Grease a 7-cup baking dish that fits in the pressure cooker. Pour mixture into dish and cover with a piece of aluminum foil. Wrap entire dish with foil in a tent-fashion, sealing all the edges well; make sure seal is watertight, but allows for some expansion.

Place dish in the steamer basket or on the trivet in cooker and add water. Seal cooker, bring up to medium pressure, reduce heat to stabilize pressure and cook for about 65 minutes.

Remove cooker from heat and release pressure. Insert a knife into the center of bread. If knife comes out clean, bread is done. If bread needs more cooking, repressurize and cook for 5 to 10 additional minutes. Turn dish upside down on a cooling rack. Remove dish from bread and cool before slicing.

CRANBERRY CHUTNEY

Instead of serving canned cranberry sauce with your holiday turkey, consider using this delicious cranberry chutney as a delightful alternative. It also makes a delicious spread for a turkey sandwich on a croissant with a little cream cheese. Since cranberries freeze well, buy several bags when they are in season and freeze them to use later.

1 cup water
4 cups fresh cranberries
½ cup dark raisins
½ cup golden raisins
2 cups sugar

1 tsp. ground ginger
1 tsp. cinnamon
½ tsp. ground allspice
½ tsp. salt
1 can (16 oz.) crushed pineapple, drained

Bring all ingredients to a boil in the pressure cooker, stirring constantly. Seal cooker, bring up to high pressure, reduce heat to stabilize pressure and cook for 5 minutes.

Remove cooker from heat and release pressure using the *Cold Water Release Method* (see page 5). Immediately remove chutney from cooker. Cool chutney to room temperature and refrigerate until ready to serve.

DESSERTS

ABOUT PRESSURE COOKING DESSERTS

- Many baked desserts can be pressure cooked, especially those that use eggs and/or are cooked over a water bath, such as custards, bread puddings and cheesecakes.

- Make sure that the dish you use to cook the dessert will fit inside the pressure cooker with at least an inch of space to spare around the edge. The larger models of pressure cookers are especially useful for making desserts.

- Seal the dish completely with foil to keep the liquid from seeping into the dessert.

- If water has accumulated on top of the foil during cooking, soak it up with a paper towel before removing the foil.

- For easy removal, place the covered dish in the steamer basket. Or, make a sling out of aluminum foil to help remove the dish from the pressure cooker.

- If not using the steamer basket, place the baking dish on the trivet to avoid burning the bottom.

- When adapting dessert recipes, be sure to use the minimum amount of liquid for cooking specified by the manufacturer. Estimate the cooking time by imitating a similar recipe in this book.

RHUBARB OATMEAL CRISP

Here's an old-fashioned treat that my grandmother used to make for me. Serve it with cinnamon-flavored whipped cream or ice cream. If rhubarb is not available, substitute your favorite berries. To toast oats, place on a baking sheet under the broiler until lightly browned, stirring frequently.

3 cups chopped rhubarb
3 tbs. all-purpose flour
1 cup granulated sugar
1 cup rolled oats, toasted
1 cup brown sugar, packed

1½ cups all-purpose flour
½ tsp. cinnamon
½ cup butter, cut into pieces
1 cup hot water

Grease a 2-quart baking dish that fits in the pressure cooker. Place rhubarb in dish and sprinkle with 3 tbs. flour and granulated sugar. In a separate bowl, combine oats, brown sugar, 1½ cups flour and cinnamon. With a pastry blender or 2 knives, cut in butter until crumbly; pat mixture over rhubarb. Cover entire dish with aluminum foil, sealing the edges well. Place dish on the trivet in pressure cooker and add water. Seal cooker, bring up to high pressure, reduce heat to stabilize pressure and cook for 20 minutes.

Heat broiler. Remove cooker from heat and release pressure. Remove foil and place dish under broiler until top is lightly browned, about 1 to 2 minutes.

PEAR BERRY OAT CRISP

Servings: 6

Pears are delicious in a crisp, especially when mixed with berries. What makes this even better is the fact that it is low in sugar! Toasting the oats greatly enhances the flavor. For instructions, see page 145.

1½ cups cooking pears, pared and sliced
2 cups raspberries
⅓ cup dried currants or raisins
⅓ cup maple syrup
2 tbs. arrowroot or cornstarch
2 tbs. lemon juice
1 cup rolled oats, toasted
¼ cup honey
½ tsp. nutmeg
½ tsp. cinnamon
¼ tsp. ground cardamom
3 tbs. butter, softened
1 cup hot water
sweetened whipped cream or vanilla ice cream, optional

Lightly coat a casserole dish that fits in the pressure cooker with nonstick cooking spray. Place pears in dish and cover with raspberries and currants. Mix maple syrup, arrowroot and lemon juice together and drizzle over pear mixture. In a separate bowl, combine oats, honey, nutmeg, cinnamon and cardamom. With a pastry blender or 2 knives, cut in butter until crumbly. Sprinkle mixture over fruits. Cover entire dish with aluminum foil, sealing the edges well. Place dish on the trivet in pressure cooker. Add water. Seal cooker, bring up to high pressure, reduce heat to stabilize pressure and cook for 10 minutes.

Heat broiler. Remove cooker from heat and release pressure. Remove foil and place dish under broiler until top is lightly browned. If desired, serve with a little sweetened whipped cream or ice cream.

APPLE CRISP

This is a perfect comforting dessert for those long winter months. During summer, substitute peaches or nectarines for apples. See page 145 for instructions on toasting oats.

3-4 large apples, prefer Golden Delicious
¾ cup brown sugar, packed
½ cup rolled oats, toasted
3 tbs. all-purpose flour
½ tsp. cinnamon
pinch salt

1 tbs. grated fresh lemon peel (zest)
¼ tsp. nutmeg
¼ cup butter
⅓ cup chopped nuts
1½ cups hot water
ice cream or sweetened whipped cream

Butter a 6-cup baking dish that fits in the pressure cooker. Peel, core and thinly slice apples. Mix together brown sugar, oats, flour, cinnamon, salt, lemon peel and nutmeg. With a pastry blender or 2 knives, cut butter into dry ingredients until crumbly. Stir in nuts. Mix about ¼ of the oat mixture with apples and place in prepared dish. Top with remaining oat mixture. Tightly cover entire dish with foil, sealing the edges well, and place in the steamer basket in pressure cooker; add water. Seal cooker, bring up to high pressure, reduce heat to stabilize pressure and cook for 20 minutes.

Heat broiler. Remove cooker from heat and release pressure. Remove foil and place dish under broiler until top is lightly browned. Serve with ice cream or whipped cream.

OLD-FASHIONED BREAD PUDDING

Servings: 6

Bread pudding stimulates good memories of home on cold winter days, and this warm pudding smothered in raisins is about as homey as it gets. Toasting the bread gives the pudding a nutty flavor.

5 cups bread cubes, toasted
5 cups heated milk
1 cup raisins
4 eggs
1½ cups sugar
½ tsp. cinnamon

⅛ tsp. nutmeg
1½ tsp. vanilla extract
¼ cup butter, melted
pinch salt
1 cup hot water

Butter a 6-cup baking dish that fits in the pressure cooker. Place bread cubes, milk and raisins in a bowl and let sit for 15 minutes. Beat eggs; add sugar, cinnamon, nutmeg, vanilla, melted butter and salt. Add egg mixture to soaked bread mixture and pour into prepared baking dish. Cover entire dish with foil, sealing the edges well, and place on the trivet in pressure cooker. Add water. Seal cooker, bring up to high pressure, reduce heat to stabilize pressure and cook for 20 minutes.

Heat broiler if desired. Remove cooker from heat and release pressure. Remove foil from dish and let pudding stand for at least 15 minutes before serving. For a crisp top, place dish under broiler for a few minutes.

SPICED PUMPKIN BREAD PUDDING

Servings: 6

Pumpkin invariably brings to mind good holiday memories. Toasting the bread before baking always gives bread pudding a better flavor.

⅔ cup sugar
2 eggs
4 egg yolks
1 cup milk
⅔ cup pumpkin puree
1 tbs. brandy, optional
1 tsp. vanilla extract
⅛ tsp. cinnamon
pinch ground ginger
pinch nutmeg
⅛ tsp. salt
5-6 slices cinnamon-raisin or egg bread, cut into cubes and toasted
2 cups hot water
sweetened whipped cream with a pinch each of cinnamon and nutmeg for garnish

Butter a 6-cup baking dish that fits in the pressure cooker. Beat sugar with eggs and egg yolks until light yellow in color. Add milk, pumpkin, brandy, if using, vanilla, cinnamon, ginger, nutmeg and salt; beat well. Place toasted bread cubes in prepared dish. Pour egg mixture over bread cubes, making sure all bread is completely covered with egg mixture.

Completely cover baking dish with aluminum foil, sealing the edges well, and place in the steamer basket in cooker. Add water. Seal cooker, bring to high pressure, reduce heat to stabilize pressure and cook for 20 minutes.

Heat broiler if desired. Remove cooker from heat and release pressure. Carefully remove foil. Let pudding stand for at least 10 minutes before serving. Garnish with flavored whipped cream. For a crisp top, place dish under broiler for a few minutes.

CHOCOLATE BREAD PUDDING

Bread pudding is an easy dessert and a good way to use up dry bread. Consider adding a light drizzle of your favorite chocolate sauce with a garnish of whipped cream for a touch of elegance, or sprinkle with toasted chopped nuts.

4 cups whole milk, heated
1 cup sugar
4 cups small bread cubes, toasted
2 oz. unsweetened chocolate, melted
2 whole eggs

2 egg yolks
1 tsp. vanilla extract, or 1 tbs. rum or
    chocolate liqueur
2 cups hot water

Butter a 2-quart baking dish that fits in the pressure cooker. Mix milk with sugar until dissolved. Pour 1/2 of the milk mixture over bread cubes and mix remaining mixture with melted chocolate. Add eggs, egg yolks and vanilla to chocolate mixture, stirring well. Gently combine egg mixture with bread cubes and pour into prepared dish. Cover entire dish with foil, sealing the edges well. Place covered dish on the trivet or in the steamer basket in cooker. Add water. Seal cooker, bring up to high pressure, reduce heat to stabilize pressure and cook for 20 minutes.

Heat broiler if desired. Remove cooker from heat and release pressure. For a crisp top, remove foil and place dish under broiler for a few minutes. Chill until set.

BROWN SUGAR RAISIN PUDDING

The boiling water poured on top becomes a brown sugar sauce, which is spooned over the cooked pudding.

1¼ cups brown sugar, packed
1 cup all-purpose flour
1 cup raisins
2 tsp. baking powder
½ tsp. salt
½ cup milk

¼ cup butter, melted
¾ tsp. cinnamon
½ tsp. nutmeg
2 cups boiling water
whipped cream or vanilla ice cream

Grease a 1½-quart baking dish that fits in the pressure cooker. In a bowl, mix together ¼ cup of the brown sugar, flour, raisins, baking powder, salt, milk and 2 tbs. of the melted butter. Pour mixture into prepared dish. In another bowl, mix together remaining 1 cup brown sugar, 2 tbs. melted butter, cinnamon, nutmeg and boiling water. Pour over raisin mixture; do not stir. Cover entire dish with aluminum foil, sealing the edges well. Place on the trivet in pressure cooker. Seal cooker, bring up to high pressure, reduce heat to stabilize pressure and cook for 22 minutes.

Remove cooker from heat and release pressure. Serve pudding warm with whipped cream or ice cream.

TRADITIONAL PLUM PUDDING

Serve this rich, spiced holiday dessert with delicious Eggnog Sauce.

granulated sugar for dusting
8 oz. pitted dates
8 oz. dried figs
8 oz. dried apricots
½ lb. walnuts, chopped
16 oz. raisins or currants
4 oz. candied citron or maraschino
    cherries
1 cup sifted all-purpose flour

1 tbs. pumpkin pie spice
1 tsp. salt
4 eggs
1 cup brown sugar, packed
½ lb. ground suet
2½ cups soft white breadcrumbs
½ cup brandy
½ cup corn syrup
2 cups hot water

Butter a 10-cup pudding mold or deep stainless steel bowl that fits in the pressure cooker and dust with sugar. Chop dates, figs and apricots into small pieces and mix with walnuts, raisins and citron. Mix together flour, pumpkin pie spice and salt; set aside. Beat eggs and brown sugar with an electric mixer for 3 minutes on high speed, until fluffy. Reduce speed to low and mix in suet, breadcrumbs, brandy and corn syrup. Stir in flour mixture until well blended. Pour mixture over fruits and nuts; stir until well blended. Pour into prepared mold, cover top with buttered waxed paper and seal with mold lid or aluminum foil fastened with string to hold tightly.

Set mold on the trivet in cooker and add water. Seal cooker, bring up to high pressure, reduce heat to stabilize pressure and cook for 1½ to 2 hours; cooking time will depend on the width and depth of mold.

Remove cooker from heat and release pressure. Check for doneness by inserting a long skewer in the center of pudding. If the skewer comes out clean, the pudding is done. If the pudding is not done, repressurize and test again in 15-minute intervals, adding more water as necessary. Cool cooked pudding in mold for 30 minutes. Loosen pudding around the edges and invert onto a wire rack. Serve with *Eggnog Sauce*.

EGGNOG SAUCE

Makes: 2 cups

2 egg yolks
½ cup sugar
1 tbs. all-purpose flour
pinch salt

2 tbs. heavy cream
¼ cup butter, softened
2 tbs. brandy
½ cup heavy cream

Beat egg yolks and sugar in the top of a double boiler until thick and lemon-colored. Stir in flour, salt and 2 tbs. cream. Cook over simmering water, adding butter 1 tablespoon at a time, and stir constantly until sauce thickens. Remove from heat, add brandy, cover and chill. Beat ½ cup cream until stiff and fold into chilled egg yolk mixture.

SOUR CREAM PUMPKIN CHEESECAKE

Even cheesecakes can be cooked in a pressure cooker! This is a delicious, delicately flavored recipe. To avoid a soggy crust due to the moisture in pressure cooking, I use just a sprinkling of crumbs to ensure easy separation from the cake pan.

½ cup graham cracker crumbs
16 oz. cream cheese, softened
1 cup brown sugar, packed
1 can (16 oz.) solid-pack pumpkin,
    about 1¾ cups
scant tbs. cornstarch
1 tsp. cinnamon
½ tsp. nutmeg
¼ tsp. ground ginger
4 eggs
1½ cups hot water
1½ cups sour cream
1 tsp. vanilla extract
¼ cup granulated sugar

Butter an 8-inch springform pan that fits in the pressure cooker and sprinkle bottom with graham cracker crumbs. With a food processor or mixer, process cream cheese until smooth. Add brown sugar, pumpkin, cornstarch, cinnamon, nutmeg and ginger; process until well blended. Add eggs one at a time, processing well after each addition. Pour mixture into prepared pan, cover mixture with waxed paper and cover entire pan tightly with aluminum foil, sealing the edges well. Pour water in cooker. Place pan in the steamer basket in pressure cooker. Seal cooker, bring up to high pressure, reduce heat to stabilize pressure and cook for 45 to 50 minutes.

Remove cooker from heat and release pressure. Check for doneness by inserting a knife in the center of cheesecake. If knife comes out clean, cake is done. If not done, repressurize and cook for a few additional minutes.

Heat oven to 350°. Mix sour cream, vanilla and sugar together and pour over cooked cheesecake. Bake in oven for 8 minutes, until topping is set. Cool cake completely; refrigerate for at least 8 hours before eating.

NOTE: You may wish to make an aluminum foil strip to use as a sling to help remove springform pan from steamer basket.

CHOCOLATE MOUSSE CHEESECAKE

This creamy cheesecake tastes like chocolate mousse. I add a hint of cinnamon to the chocolate crumbs — it drives people crazy because they can't quite figure out what's in there.

½ cup chocolate wafer crumbs
pinch cinnamon
8 oz. semisweet chocolate
1 tbs. butter
16 oz. cream cheese, softened
1 cup heavy cream
1 tsp. vanilla extract
⅔ cup sugar
2 eggs, beaten
1½ tbs. unsweetened cocoa powder
1½ cups water
confectioners' sugar for garnish, optional
whipped cream for garnish, optional
sliced strawberries for garnish, optional

Grease an 8-inch springform pan that fits in the pressure cooker. Mix chocolate crumbs and cinnamon together and sprinkle on the bottom of springform pan, pressing gently. Melt chocolate and butter together and set aside. With a food processor or mixer, process cream cheese until smooth. Add chocolate mixture and process until mixture is well mixed and uniformly colored. Add cream, vanilla, sugar and eggs, beating well. Sieve cocoa powder over batter and pulse or mix on low speed until cocoa is thoroughly incorporated. Pour mixture over crumbs in pan. Cover cake with a piece of waxed paper. Cover entire pan with aluminum foil, sealing the edges well. Add water to cooker. Place pan on the trivet in pressure cooker. Seal cooker, bring up to high pressure, reduce heat to stabilize pressure and cook for 45 to 50 minutes.

Remove cooker from heat and release pressure. Cool cheesecake to room temperature in pan on a rack. Remove cheesecake from pan and refrigerate for 8 hours before serving. If desired, garnish with confectioners' sugar, or whipped cream and sliced strawberries.

PEARS IN WINE

If you are looking for a light dessert, especially after a heavy winter meal, consider a yummy wine-drenched pear filled with a crunchy cookie filling.

6 firm cooking pears
1 cup sugar
½ tsp. grated fresh lemon peel (zest)
2 cups dry red wine
1½ tsp. cornstarch
1½ tsp. water
½ cup chopped almonds
2 tbs. sugar
2-3 macaroons, vanilla wafers or
    toasted ladyfingers, crushed
whipped cream for garnish

Peel pears and cut a thin slice from pear bottoms so they will stand upright. Remove cores with an apple corer. Mix together 1 cup sugar, lemon peel and wine. Place pears upright on trivet in pressure cooker so they will not to fall over. Pour wine mixture over pears and bring to a boil. Seal cooker, bring up to high pressure, reduce heat to stabilize pressure and cook for about 15 minutes, depending on the size and firmness of pears.

Remove cooker from heat and release pressure. Carefully remove pears and refrigerate until cool.

Cook wine mixture uncovered in pressure cooker over high heat for about 6 to 8 minutes, until slightly reduced. Dissolve cornstarch in water and add to boiling wine mixture; stir until thickened. Cool sauce slightly and pour over cold pears; place pears in the refrigerator and chill until sauce adheres to pears as a glaze. Repeat glazing process 1 to 2 times until pears are nicely glazed. Mix together almonds, 2 tbs. sugar and macaroons into fine crumbs. Place pears in serving dishes and fill cavities with almond mixture. Pour any remaining sauce over pears and garnish with whipped cream.

ALMOND MERINGUE-STUFFED PEACHES IN RASPBERRY SAUCE

This recipe is similar to peach melba, but with a tasty, crunchy filling. It's a refreshing dessert after a heavy meal. Depending on the appetite of your guests, serve either 1 or 2 peach halves per person.

6 ripe peaches
1 cup water
2 egg whites
¼ cup sugar
1 cup vanilla wafer crumbs
½ cup chopped toasted almonds

2 tbs. amaretto
Raspberry Sauce, follows
mint sprigs for garnish, optional
sweetened whipped cream for garnish,
  optional

Peel peaches, cut in half and remove pits. Place peach halves in the steamer basket or on the trivet in the pressure cooker. Add water and bring to a boil. Seal cooker, bring up to high pressure and immediately remove from heat and release pressure. Transfer peach halves to a baking dish with the cavities facing up.

Heat broiler. With a mixer, beat eggs whites until soft peaks form. Add sugar and beat until stiff peaks form. Fold in wafer crumbs, toasted almonds and amaretto. Spoon egg white mixture onto peach halves, covering cut surface entirely. Broil about 6 inches from heat source until golden brown, about 3 to 5 minutes; watch closely so meringue doesn't burn.

Spoon a little *Raspberry Sauce* on the bottom of each serving plate and place 1 or 2 peach halves on top. Garnish with a sprig of mint and a small dollop of whipped cream if desired.

RASPBERRY SAUCE
Makes: 1 cup

1 pkg. (10 oz.) frozen raspberries,
    thawed
few drops lemon juice

½ cup sugar, or more to taste
2 tbs. raspberry or amaretto liqueur,
    optional

Puree raspberries with a blender or food processor with lemon juice and sugar. Taste and adjust sweetness. Sieve berry mixture to remove seeds and add liqueur, if using.

FANTASTIC FLAN

Using 3 types of milk creates an incredibly creamy texture. A properly cooked flan usually takes hours of slow cooking at low temperatures. This wonderfully simple and delicious recipe only takes 20 minutes.

1/2 cup sugar
6 egg yolks
1 can (14 oz.) sweetened condensed milk
1 can (12 oz.) evaporated milk
1 cup whole milk
1 tsp. vanilla extract
1 cup hot water
1 cup whipped cream
1 tbs. sugar
1/4 tsp. cinnamon

In a heavy-bottomed saucepan, cook sugar over medium heat, stirring, until it melts and begins to turn golden brown. Immediately remove from heat and pour into a 6-cup baking dish that fits in the pressure cooker. Rotate dish to evenly spread caramelized sugar and let stand until caramel has hardened.

With a food processor, blender or mixer, beat egg yolks well. Add evaporated milk, condensed milk, whole milk and vanilla; mix well. Pour mixture over caramel in dish. Cover entire dish with aluminum foil, sealing the edges well. Pour water into cooker. Place covered dish in pressure cooker on the trivet. Seal cooker, bring up to high pressure, reduce heat to stabilize pressure and cook for 20 minutes.

Remove cooker from heat and release pressure. Immediately remove flan from cooker. Remove foil, cool flan to room temperature and refrigerate until firm. Invert flan onto a rimmed serving dish, letting caramel drip over the edges. Mix whipped cream with sugar and cinnamon and use to garnish flan.

EGG CUSTARD

As children, we used to beg our mother to make this dessert. With a pressure cooker it only takes 10 minutes to cook. Substitute freshly grated lemon peel, orange peel or even dry sherry in place of the vanilla for a delightful change.

2 eggs
1 egg yolk
½ cup sugar
¼ tsp. salt

2 cups milk
1 tsp. vanilla extract
generous amount nutmeg
1½ cups hot water

In a bowl, whisk together eggs, egg yolk, sugar and salt. In a saucepan, heat milk over high heat until steaming; do not boil. Remove from heat and stir into egg mixture along with vanilla. Pour into a 1-quart baking dish that fits in the pressure cooker and sprinkle with nutmeg. Cover custard with a piece of waxed paper and cover entire dish with aluminum foil, sealing the edges well. Add water. Place dish in the steamer basket or on trivet in cooker. Seal cooker, bring up to high pressure, reduce heat to stabilize pressure and cook for 10 minutes.

Remove cooker from heat and release pressure. Remove dish and let custard stand for at least 15 minutes before serving. Serve either warm or chilled.

INDEX

Serve Creative, Easy, Nutritious Meals with nitty gritty® Cookbooks

100 Dynamite Desserts
The 9 x 13 Pan Cookbook
The Barbecue Cookbook
Beer and Good Food
The Best Bagels are Made at Home
The Best Pizza is Made at Home
The Big Book of Bread Machine Recipes
Blender Drinks
Bread Baking
Bread Machine Cookbook
Bread Machine Cookbook II
Bread Machine Cookbook III
Bread Machine Cookbook IV
Bread Machine Cookbook V
Bread Machine Cookbook VI
The Little Burger Bible
Cappuccino/Espresso
Casseroles
The Coffee Book
Convection Oven Cookery
The Cook-Ahead Cookbook
Cooking for 1 or 2
Cooking in Clay

Cooking in Porcelain
Cooking on the Indoor Grill
Cooking with Chile Peppers
Cooking with Grains
Cooking with Your Kids
The Dehydrator Cookbook
Edible Pockets for Every Meal
Entrees from Your Bread Machine
Extra-Special Crockery Pot Recipes
Fabulous Fiber Cookery
Fondue and Hot Dips
Fresh Vegetables
From Freezer, 'Fridge and Pantry
From Your Ice Cream Maker
The Garlic Cookbook
Gourmet Gifts
Healthy Cooking on the Run
Healthy Snacks for Kids
The Juicer Book
The Juicer Book II
Lowfat American Favorites
New International Fondue Cookbook
No Salt, No Sugar, No Fat

One-Dish Meals
The Pasta Machine Cookbook
Pinch of Time: Meals in Less than 30
    Minutes
Quick and Easy Pasta Recipes
Recipes for the Loaf Pan
Recipes for the Pressure Cooker
Recipes for Yogurt Cheese
Risottos, Paellas, and other Rice
    Specialties
Rotisserie Oven Cooking
The Sandwich Maker Cookbook
The Sensational Skillet: Sautés and Stir-Fries
Slow Cooking in Crock-Pot,® Slow Cooker,
    Oven and Multi-Cooker
Soups and Stews
The Toaster Oven Cookbook
Unbeatable Chicken Recipes
The Vegetarian Slow Cooker
New Waffles and Pizzelles
Wraps and Roll-Ups

For a free catalog, call: Bristol Publishing Enterprises, Inc.
(800) 346-4889
www.bristolcookbooks.com